GRILL IT!

GRILL IT!

RECIPES • TECHNIQUES • TOOLS

CHRIS SCHLESINGER
& JOHN WILLOUGHBY

LONDON NEW YORK MELBOURNE
MUNICH DELHI

Produced for Dorling Kindersley by

cobaltid

The Stables, Wood Farm, Deopham Road,
Attleborough, Norfolk NR17 1AJ
www.cobaltid.co.uk

ART EDITORS
Paul Reid, Lloyd Tilbury,
Darren Bland, Claire Dale

EDITORS
Louise Abbott,
Marek Walisiewicz, Kati Dye,

PHOTOGRAPHY ART DIRECTION
Paul Reid

FOOD STYLIST
Gizzi Erskine

PHOTOGRAPHY
Ian O'Leary, with assistance
from Gemma Reynolds

For Dorling Kindersley

MANAGING EDITOR
Dawn Henderson

MANAGING ART EDITOR
Heather McCarry

EDITOR
Ariane Durkin

PROJECT ART EDITOR
Caroline de Souza

PRODUCTION EDITOR
Luca Frassinetti

PRODUCTION CONTROLLER
Mandy Inness

AMERICANIZATION EDITOR
Anja Schmidt

First American Edition, 2008

Published in the United States by
DK Publishing
375 Hudson Street
New York, New York 10014

08 09 10 11 10 9 8 7 6 5 4 3 2 1

GD048 Mar-08

Published in Great Britain by Dorling Kindersley Ltd.

A catalog record for this book is available from the Library of Congress.

ISBN 978-0-7566-1741-7

DK books are available at special discounts when purchased in bulk for sales promotions,
premiums, fund-raising, or educational use. For details contact: DK Publishing Special Markets,
375 Hudson Street, New York, New York 10014 or SpecialSales@dk.com

Printed and bound by Hing Hung, China

Discover more at

www.dk.com

CONTENTS

FIRING UP

COOKING OVER LIVE FIRE IS FUN. BUT TO BE TRULY RELAXED AND CAREFREE AT THE GRILL, YOU NEED TO KNOW HOW TO DO A FEW THINGS: CHOOSE YOUR FUEL AND YOUR TOOLS, BUILD AND START THE FIRE, DECIDE WHEN YOUR FOOD IS DONE, AND ADD EVEN MORE FLAVOR TO IT. READ ON.

WHAT IS GRILLING?

We love grilling, because it's the most direct and straightforward of all cooking methods: You put some food over a fire and leave it there until it's cooked. So grilling appeals to us on an almost instinctual level—after all, we humans have been doing it pretty much since we climbed down from the trees. But the other thing that draws us to grilling (in addition, of course, to the wonderful flavor it gives to food) is that, despite its simplicity, it is also intriguingly complex. Each live fire you build is a little bit different from any other one that ever existed. This means that you have to pay attention—you have to react with that particular fire and the particular food you are cooking. So the process involves not only the atavistic joy of playing with fire, but also the appeal of a game that's just slightly different every time you play it. And it's even more than that.

To fully plumb the nature of this technique, it makes sense to look at it from three points of view, taking the best from each along the way. To most Americans, for example, grilling is not just a way of cooking food, it's a central part of a near-mythic social ritual known as the backyard cookout. This culinary rite forms an important part of the American self-image, and as such is characterized by what are thought of as prototypically American attributes: casualness, informality, equality, and a kind of genial, low-key camaraderie. To underline the carefree, democratic nature of the occasion, the grilling at cookouts has traditionally been performed by dads, who at other times have tended to treat cooking as a foreign realm of endeavor. From this American model, grillers can take what is perhaps the single most important aspect of the method: It's just plain fun. But grilling has a long and distinguished history that far predates the US. It is, in fact, a highly respected, bona fide cooking technique with a pedigree supplied by no less than Auguste Escoffier, the 19th-century French master chef who codified culinary techniques as practiced in the West. In his seminal book, *Ma Cuisine*, Escoffier recognized grilling as "the remote starting point, the very genesis of our art."

But what should go over the flames? Although this has changed over the last couple of decades, the American idea of grilling food traditionally ran to burgers, steaks, and hot dogs—the type of food that even a novice dad had a fair chance of getting right. Escoffier was more adventuresome, but leaned toward chops, steaks, and fish fillets draped in complex sauces. Fortunately, the cuisines of the hot-weather world contain a massive repertoire of imaginative grilled food. Even today, for a great many home cooks in these regions, cooking over live fire is neither a weekend ritual nor a professional technique—it's simply the way they cook every day. And they've been doing it for hundreds of years.

Here, then, grillers can find a whole new world of possibilities. Watching a fisherman grill freshly-caught sardines on a beach in southern Portugal, savoring skewers of grilled lamb in a side street in Istanbul or spicy shrimp in a market in Saigon, munching on a crisp, flame-marked pappadum in Bombay, or sitting down to a Middle Eastern *meze* with its grilled peppers, tomatoes, and eggplant, you realize that the possibilities for grilled food are virtually endless.

And there you have it. By extracting the best points from three distinct approaches, the modern griller becomes multidimensional— relaxed and casual but technically expert and imaginative in menu choices. And, of course, you get to play with fire. So let's get grilling.

YOUR LIVE FIRE REPERTOIRE

People all over the world routinely cook with live fire, and they use all kinds of inventive methods when they do so. We think it's not only interesting but useful to know the differences between these various techniques. The best way to understand them, to us, is to look at what is being cooked, what temperature it is being cooked at, and why this method is the appropriate one for that food. In other words, it's good to understand the methods by looking at what you're trying to achieve.

GRILLING

Grilling basically involves cooking food quickly over the coals of a hot fire. When food is laid over the direct heat of the coals, a seared crust develops on the exterior. This flavor-packed crust (not the fuel) is most directly responsible for the characteristic taste of grilled food. On the other hand, the food also needs to be properly cooked on

The lid stays open for direct-heat cooking

A thick layer of coals will give you the intense heat you need

If cooking thick or bone-in cuts, tapering the coals toward the fire edge gives you an area of gentler heat to get interior doneness right without over-charring the outside

Coal-free area gives you somewhere to move food to in case of flare-ups

A FIRE FOR SIMPLE GRILLING

Depending on what you're planning to cook, you'll need to build either a simple or a multilevel fire (see p30). Start checking the temperature (see p34) as soon as the flames die down to catch the right moment to cook.

GRILLING: THE FACTS

- Fire temperature depends on what is being cooked
- Fast cooking, lid open
- What to grill: Small, tender things; steaks, chops, baby back ribs; fish fillets, fish steaks, and other seafood; vegetables and fruits

SAMPLE RECIPES 1. Rosemary-Grilled New York Strip Steak (*p60*); 2. Asian-Flavored Baby Back Pork Ribs (*p88*); 3. Thai Chicken Sticks (*p210*); 4. Coriander-Crusted Grilled Halibut Steaks (*p120*); 5. Grilled Clams (*p140*).

the inside by the time it comes off the grill. This relationship between surface sear and interior doneness, then, becomes the crux of the matter, the key to great grilled food. These are our top tips for perfect grilling:

- Build the right fire (*see pp30–1*) for the food you're going to grill.
- Before you put that food on the grill, be sure that you are cooking with the right temperature fire. Not everything should be cooked over the same heat, so always check the recipe and then see how hot the fire is (*see p34*) before you start cooking.
- Never cover the grill when you're doing direct-heat grilling (*see p35*).
- Start checking food for doneness (*see pp36–7*) well before you think it is actually ready to come off the grill. All live fires are different, so cooking times in recipes are just approximations, and checking for doneness early and often just may save you from a dry, overcooked dinner.

BARBECUING

This is where the terminology can be confusing. In much of the English-speaking world, including large parts of the United States, "barbecuing" and "grilling" are used interchangeably. But in the South and Texas, "barbecue" describes a cooking method in which food is cooked slowly over the indirect heat and smoke from a charcoal or

hardwood fire, which is quite different from cooking directly over the coals. The term is also used to describe the meat cooked by this method, which should always be both tender and smoky if you've done it right. Like braising, barbecuing was developed to deal with large, tough pieces of meat that need slow cooking over low heat in order to become tender. The best-known examples are the pork shoulder, favored by North Carolina fans; beef brisket, the most popular barbecue of Texas; lamb shoulder, which you'll find most prominently in Kentucky; and ribs, which are found all through the southern half of the country.

The temperature of a barbecue pit should be somewhere between 180 and 240°F (80–115°C). As the meat basks in the low, smoky

USING THE GRILL TO BARBECUE As the food is not directly above the coals, you don't, when the lid is closed, get a buildup of the acrid fumes caused when fat drips onto the fire (*see also p35*), so the barbecue won't be tainted by off flavors.

Heap the coals well up to one side of the grill. You don't need a lot of charcoal to produce gentle barbecuing heat

The food is always placed over the coal-free area

Closing the lid creates an oven-like cooking environment

Partially open the vents to keep the fire going yet retain the heat

BARBECUING: THE FACTS

- Low heat (180–240°F/ 80–115°C)
- Slow cooking, lid on
- What to cook: Large, tough cuts of meat— racks of ribs, shoulder joints, beef brisket

SAMPLE RECIPES
1. North Carolina-Style Pulled Pork Barbecue (*p196*) 2. Texas-Style Slow Beef Brisket (*p180*) 3. Cuban Ribs (*p46*).

heat, the tough connecting tissue in the meat—known as collagen—dissolves, and the meat itself goes from very tough to extremely tender. The technique of barbecuing involves building a fire on only one side of your grill, using about enough charcoal to fill a large shoebox, then putting the food on the other side and covering the grill. After that you just let it cook, adding a handful of coals every 30 minutes or so to keep the temperature in the proper range.

The technique of barbecuing is simple, requiring primarily patience, but it gives a remarkable end result, as generations of Southern barbecue cooks can testify. One more thing while we're talking barbecue: You don't use temperature to decide when your barbecue is ready to eat, because you are looking to go beyond mere doneness all the way to tenderness. Instead, use the "fork test": Stick a large fork into whatever you're cooking and try to pick it up. If the fork slides out of the meat without grabbing onto it, it's done; otherwise, keep cooking.

TOPPING OFF THE FIRE "Little and often" is the secret to keeping a good, slow barbecuing fire going. Some barbecue takes 8 hours or more to cook, so be sure to lay in a good supply of charcoal to take you through the day (or night).

SMOKE-ROASTING

Next to grilling itself, this is the most useful of the live-fire cooking methods. It is similar to barbecuing, but you are cooking at a higher temperature, between 300 and 450°F (150–230°C). So when you build the fire on one side of your grill you use more charcoal than when barbecuing, enough to fill about 1½ shoeboxes, and when you add charcoal during refueling, you use two handfuls rather than one. Basically what you are doing is roasting in a smoky environment. Like oven roasting, this method is most

Closing the lid keeps all that heat inside to roast the food

The joint or bird sits over the coal-free half of the grill, preventing fat flare-ups and acrid fumes

suitable for large, relatively tender foods—beef and pork roasts, leg of lamb, fresh ham, chickens, turkeys, ducks, whole fish, and basically anything else you would put in the oven if you were cooking inside. But you have the additional advantage that whatever you're cooking will pick up that ineffable smoky flavor from the charcoal or wood you're burning.

SMOKE-ROASTING ON THE GRILL
A deep layer of coals over half the base of the grill (*see left and top of page*) gives you your initial high heat; to keep this going, you need to top the fire off generously every half-hour or so.

SMOKE-ROASTING: THE FACTS

- Hot fire (300–450°F/ 150–230°C)
- Medium to long cooking times, lid on
- What to cook: Large but tender, juicy joints; whole birds and fish

SAMPLE RECIPES 1. Glazed Smoke-Roasted Fresh Ham (*p204*) 2. Smoke-Roasted Whole Duck (*p200*); 3. Pepper-Crusted Smoke-Roasted Top Loin (*p194*).

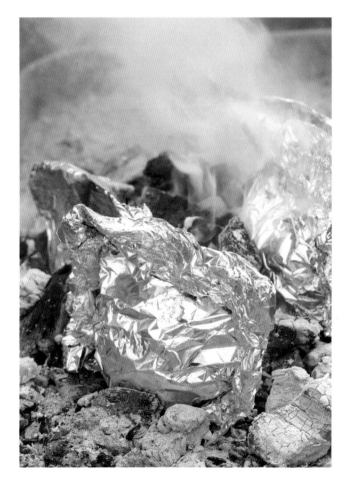

ASH-ROASTING IN FOIL Lots of vegetables grill well, but ash-roasting gives your side dishes a melting, succulent texture to contrast with the seared crust of a grilled steak or chop.

ASH-ROASTING

Since ancient times, people have been encasing food in leaves and putting it in a pit with coals to cook. It is still fairly widely used today—think of the Hawaiian *luau* or the *pibil* of Mexico. Ash-roasting, also known as "hobo pack cooking" (the Boy Scout name for it), is really just a variation on this method. Instead of leaves, you wrap the food in foil; instead of a coal-lined pit, you simply slide it into the coals of your fire. It's pretty much as simple as that, but there are two important things to remember. First, be sure that there is a good amount of liquid in the parcel; otherwise the food will dry out in those hot coals. Second, wrap the foil carefully, so that juices don't leak out. The package doesn't need to be dug down into the coals so it's completely covered. Instead, just push it in so the coals come partway up the sides. This technique is particularly useful because you can cook your side dishes—or even your dessert—in the coals while other food is cooking above them.

WHAT'S THE BEST GRILL FOR YOU?

We've grilled on a $5,000 superbehemoth gas grill, an oven rack perched on three rocks, and pretty much everything in between. And what we've learned is that the most important thing is technique, not equipment. In addition, we know that the particular grill that you choose is largely a matter of **personal preference**, **budget**, and **available space**. Having said all that, though, we have found, over many years, that there are a couple of grill qualities that can make grilling easier and more successful.

First, it is best to get **a covered grill**. While you can do a fine job grilling on a hibachi, you need that cover for any of the other live-fire cooking techniques, such as smoke-roasting or barbecuing. It's even more important to get a grill with **a generous grilling surface**. A couple of years ago I (Chris) got a giant charcoal grill, 4ft (120cm) in diameter, and I've become addicted to it. It lets me entertain a crowd without having to cook in stages. It also makes it possible to have a wide range of heat: I can be searing steaks over **a hot fire on one side**, and slow-cooking tomatoes over **a low fire on the other**, while still having a space with no coals at all in case I need to move something there to **quickly cool down**. In other words, it just gives me the most **versatility**. Of course, you may not have room in your backyard (or your budget) for a grill this giant, but we strongly recommend: When buying a grill, get the largest one you can accommodate. You need a grill grid at least **22in (55cm) across** for anything but the simplest, most direct grilling. One other feature that's worth looking for is **a grill rack with a hinged lid** so it's easy to add more charcoal during cooking—particularly useful for smoke-roasting.

WHAT TO LOOK FOR Space for tools (1) is always handy; titanic gas grills (2) often feature warming areas, too, but with a petite charcoal grill (3), a side table is a must. Rustic portables (4) have charm, but you'll find one with a vented lid gives more cooking scope; for example, a miniature version (5) of the classic kettle grill (6).

CHOOSING FUELS

The charcoal briquette is so easy to find that it is the default fuel for most grillers. And, although our top choice for fuel is always hardwood charcoal, briquettes are fine with us, too, provided that you give them time for the chemicals they contain to burn off. Hardwood logs (*see p24*) are ideal for those who love tinkering with a fire, but their unpredictability can be challenging. One of our favorite fire-building techniques is to combine charcoal with a single log (*see p30*). That way, you get the best of both fuels. Finally, of course, there's gas (*see p25*): We have to say that for us, it will never rival the joys of live-fire cooking, but there's no denying its convenience.

FUEL YOUR IMAGINATION Logs appeal to those who crave a truly primal grilling experience, but traditional hardwood charcoal also has a long and distinguished history in firebuilding.

THE REAL DEAL Hardwood charcoal certainly gives a superior grilling experience. If you can find a supplier whose charcoal comes from sustainable sources, you can feel good about that, too.

THE UBIQUITOUS BRIQUETTE These familiar little pillow shapes can be bought almost anywhere. Cheap, clean, and convenient, they can provide a good, even, and intense heat.

HARDWOOD CHARCOAL

This is the real deal, charcoal made by the traditional method, which involves burning hardwood in a closed container with very little oxygen. Because it is simply wood that has been reduced to charcoal, it comes in irregularly-shaped lumps rather than uniform briquettes. It has several advantages over briquettes, all of which derive from the fact that it is almost pure carbon—it lights a little more easily, it is more responsive to changes in oxygen level so you can regulate it more easily, and (most importantly) it burns cleaner and hotter than briquettes. Its major disadvantage is that it's more difficult to locate, plus it is slightly more expensive.

CHARCOAL BRIQUETTES

Briquettes have several advantages: You can find them anywhere, they provide a good, hot fire if you use enough of them, and they are relatively inexpensive. They do have one disadvantage, though—they are not pure charcoal. Instead, they are powdered charcoal pressed together with binders, and sometimes chemical additives so they will light more easily. The only real problem with this is that until the briquettes are completely caught, a little bit of what you are burning is chemicals. So when you use briquettes, just be sure that you don't put any food over them until all the briquettes are totally covered with gray ash.

LOG FIRE Though the heat they provide is unpredictable, logs are great fun to grill over. A single log combined with a charcoal fire, however, gives you the best of both worlds.

HERB BRANCHES Cut your own for an inexpensive way to create a Mediterranean atmosphere—but unless you're doing lid-on cookery, they won't add much flavor to the food.

HARDWOOD LOGS

Logs are, of course, the original grilling fuel. Their primary characteristics are that they burn for a long time, which is a good thing, and that they burn unevenly and unpredictably, which can be either good or bad. If you're one of those people who think tending the fire is fun, then this is the fuel for you, because there's a lot of watching and shifting around involved. We like to compromise with a "dual fuel" fire (*see* Our Favorite Fire, *p30*). It's best to use seasoned logs. Greenwood chunks and chips are great for adding a little extra aroma (*see right*), but a greenwood fire will spit and smoke too much for good grilling.

MINOR FUEL OPTIONS

Wood chips and other aromatics such as vine trimmings and dried herbs are appropriate for slower, covered techniques such as smoke-roasting or barbecuing. In those situations, the food is going to spend enough time bathed in the smoke to pick up some of its flavor characteristics. (You can even use chunky trimmings from hardwood trees in your yard, such as apple and maple; the greener they are, the more smoke they will produce.) When you are doing just straight grilling, however, all they are really doing is perfuming the air, not the food. So unless you're a big believer in aromatherapy, save these aromatics for covered cooking.

GRILLING ON GAS

The advice we've given so far, of course, all relates to charcoal grills. But let's talk for a minute about gas grills. We don't have a lot to say about them, because we don't have much experience with them. The reason is simple: We love the excitement and unpredictability of live fire, so we really don't use gas. But their speed and convenience have made gas grills increasingly popular and, while you won't get the same experience as with true live fire, it's sure a lot better than not grilling at all.

COOKING ON A GAS GRILL

Any of the recipes in this book can easily be done over a gas grill. Just be sure that you let the grill heat up for 15 minutes (with the lid closed) before you begin to cook, and set the dial to hot, medium, or low. When we call for a "multilevel fire," turn off the burner on one side or at the front or back, depending upon how your grill is configured.

A lid is essential to build up a good grilling temperature

A generous grill area is our number one requirement, whatever the fuel

Check that the grill base slopes for good drainage to minimize flare-ups

The more you spend, the more extra features for convenience you'll get, such as these wings

CHOOSING A GAS GRILL

Follow the same general rules as with a charcoal grill (see p20)—get the biggest and most powerful one you can afford and accommodate, so you'll have room to cook a lot at the same time, and get some char on your food.

Dual burners give you two temperature zones that mimic a multilevel live fire

The gas bottle will usually be enclosed or screened. Make sure there's a gauge that tells you how much fuel you have left

ESSENTIAL GRILLING TOOLS

HAVING THE RIGHT TOOLS makes any task easier, and that's true of grilling, as well. The trick is to have all the tools you actually need without cluttering up your grill with a lot of unnecessary stuff. Here's our essential list. **1. HEAVY-DUTY, LONG-HANDLED, SPRING-LOADED TONGS** The number one grill tool. Like an extra hand that doesn't get burned, they are ideal for placing food on the grill, moving it around while it's cooking, picking it up to check for doneness, and taking it off the grill. Get two or three, so you can place them strategically around the grilling area. Each qualifier is important: The tongs should be heavy-duty so they will not bend when you lift big pieces of food; have long handles so you can work over a hot fire without burning your arms; and be spring-loaded so they are always ready to use, rather than having to be opened each time. **2. WIRE BRUSH** The brushes that come with fancy grill sets are usually not as sturdy or efficient as the ones for paint-scraping that you pick up at a hardware store. They're great for cleaning the grill grid right after you finish cooking, before any grease congeals and while the hot coals will disintegrate any food residue that falls into them. This brush will be your biggest ally in the war against sticking. Since they do wear out, pick up a couple—preferably the wooden-handled variety, which are more durable. **3. DISPOSABLE FOIL PANS** These might seem an odd essential, but they have many uses. They're just the thing for carrying raw food to the grill and cooked food from grill to table. They're also ideal for covering that big, thick pork chop or bone-in chicken breast that's not quite done yet but has to stay on the cooler side of the fire to finish cooking; it allows you to create a kind of mini-oven without closing the grill lid and trapping ashy, "off" flavors. **4. THERMOMETERS** We like to keep two types

handy: A small, dial-face, instant-read thermometer for checking the interior doneness of roasts, chickens, or anything else big and bulky, and an oven thermometer to put inside the grill if it doesn't have one and you're going to smoke-roast or barbecue. **5. DOGLEG SPATULA** Much as we like tongs, there are some things—delicate fish fillets, for example—better lifted or turned with a dogleg or offset spatula with a large surface area. The dogleg feature lets you slip the blade under the food more easily, and the large surface area is important so that foods don't hang off the edges and break. **6. INEXPENSIVE KITCHEN TOWELS** Use them to pick up hot dishes or skewers—it's much quicker to grab a couple of towels than to fit your hand into a mitt. Just be sure they're not wet when you use them this way, since wet cloth is a great heat conductor. Of course, they also come in handy for spills and generally keeping your grilling environment neat. **7. SKEWERS** You'll need these for kebabs, of course, and they can be useful for small items, since threading them onto skewers keeps them from falling through the grill grid. Some folks like metal skewers because they can be reused; others prefer the convenience of disposable wooden ones. If you go with the latter, don't bother soaking them before using them; the portion of the skewer inside the food isn't going to burn, and the part outside the food will dry and burn over the fire, anyway. **8. YOUR FAVORITE BEVERAGE** Next to tongs, this may be the most indispensable grilling tool. It helps keep you cool and calm while you're tending the fire—a key to success. It also helps you keep your perspective—remember that the point of grilling is not just to cook delicious food, but also to have fun. When you're having fun, so will your guests, which means that even if something isn't cooked perfectly, dinner will still be a success. Since you don't want to be running inside to get a refill, we recommend having an ice bucket filled with Favorite Beverage right by your side. That way, you can also graciously share with guests.

BUILDING THE FIRE

You can either lay a very simple fire, basically consisting of a pile of charcoal, or a slightly more complicated, multilevel type; it all depends on what you are cooking. Use plenty of charcoal when building your fire. After all, you're spending more on the food than on the fuel, and having a fire that is large enough and hot enough is a key to good grilling.

SIMPLE ONE-LEVEL FIRE

If you are cooking something small that is easily cooked through on the inside without burning on the outside, such as a steak or a boneless chicken breast, you want to cook it directly above the coals. In that case, you can build a one-level fire, simply following the instructions on pp32–3 for lighting your fuel. We do recommend, however, that even when building this very elemental fire you leave a space in the grill bed with no coals.

OUR FAVORITE FIRE

To add a little more grilling scope to a simple fire, our very favorite technique is to shore up the charcoal with a small log. Once the coals are completely lit, position the log along the edge of the coals and use your tongs to push it across the bottom of the grill, bunching the coals up behind it. Once it catches, you'll get both the steady, predictable heat of the charcoal and the long-lasting, smoky heat of the wood.

A "dead area" with no coals gives you a place to move food to in case of flare-ups (*see p34*)

A log along the edge of your charcoal helps keep the fire going and gives smoky flavor

A MULTILEVEL FIRE gives you control when cooking something like a thick steak, where the relationship between surface sear and interior doneness needs to be finely balanced.

A GOOD-SIZED GRILL makes it far easier to lay a generous multilevel fire; the different grilling zones then allow you to cook a variety of items that need different cooking temperatures.

MULTILEVEL CHARCOAL FIRE

If you are cooking something such as a thick pork chop or a bone-in chicken breast, you need a multilevel fire. The reason is quite straightforward: If you have a fire with hotter and cooler portions, you can move food around according to whether it needs more sear on the outside (to the hot zone) or more cooking on the inside without exterior sear (to the cool zone). Laying this fire is only slightly more complicated. To do so, lay a bed of charcoal that is about 3in (7.5cm) deep on one side, tapers out to about 1in (2.5cm) on the other side, and is larger in surface area than the total surface area of the food you are planning to grill. This way, you will end up with a very hot side and a cooler side. As an alternative, you can initially build the fire in one side of the grill, then shove some of the coals over to the other side after the fire is well lit. To our way of thinking, it is so simple to lay a multilevel fire that you might as well do it as a matter of course, on the chance that you will need the various levels of heat. However, in those recipes where you are doing direct grilling only, we do not call for this. You decide.

A thick bed of coals gives fierce heat at the back, tapering to a single layer of coals for more gentle heat

STARTING THE FIRE

USING A CHIMNEY STARTER

The best tool for lighting a fire, in our opinion, is the chimney starter. It's an incredibly simple device consisting of a sheet metal cylinder, open at both ends, with a ring of ventilation holes around the bottom, a grid located inside the flue several inches from the bottom, and a handle. To use it, you just set it in the middle of the fire grate, fill the bottom section with crumpled newspaper, then fill the top with charcoal and light the newspaper. The flames will sweep up through the chimney, igniting the charcoal. When the charcoal is red-hot, which should take about five minutes, dump it out and put as much additional charcoal as you want on top of or around it. It's that quick and easy.

OTHER OPTIONS

Of course, there are other options for starting your fire. Lighter fluid, which has acquired a tarnished reputation lately, is actually an acceptable choice, provided that you wait until the coals are all lit before you start cooking (which you should do, anyway). Another reasonable option is the electric coil starter, which consists of a thick, oval electrical coil with a plastic handle. You

---

FIRELIGHTING METHODS

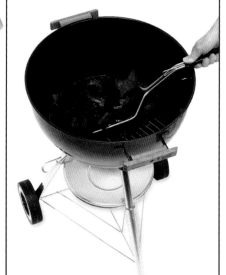

CHIMNEY STARTER Also known as a flue, this is one of those wonderful tools that is simple yet 100% effective. You just light the paper at the base—the flames are then drawn up to ignite the coals.

LIGHTER FLUID This has been criticized for imparting chemical flavors, but if you wait until the fluid is all burned off before you put anything over the fire, it won't affect the taste of the food.

ELECTRIC STARTER Once the red-hot electric element ignites the charcoal resting on it, unplug the starter and set it aside on a fireproof surface, out of reach of children, until it is cool.

WAITING TO COOK Just a few lit coals will ignite the rest; then, wait for the flames to die down. As white ash starts to cover the charcoal, the temperature will rise until all the coals are gray.

put it right on the grate, mound charcoal on top of it, and plug it into a grounded outlet; the coil will soon become red-hot, igniting the charcoal that's in contact with it.

ONCE THE FIRE IS LIT

Remember, there's no need to light all the charcoal with your starting method. As long as you get at least one piece of charcoal going, it will light the piece of charcoal next to it, which will light the ones next to it, and so on. It will take 20–30 minutes for the fire to work up to the fiery-red stage, then die down until the coals become covered with a fine, gray ash. Then, once the fire reaches the correct temperature for your food (*see overleaf*), you're ready to cook.

MANAGING YOUR FIRE

GAUGING THE TEMPERATURE

Wait until the coals are completely covered with gray ash, then hold your hand about 5in (12cm) above the grill grid. Count how many seconds you can comfortably leave it there.

1–2 seconds The fire is **hot**;
3–4 seconds You have **medium** heat;
5–6 seconds You have a **low** fire.

The fire's heat will peak when all the coals are gray, then slowly start to cool down, so start checking the temperature early. If you miss the peak of heat and need a hot fire, add more coals and wait until they are all gray.

ALL OUR GRILL RECIPES specify either a hot, medium, or low grilling heat, so to ensure success, it's important to check the fire's temperature before you put the food on the grill.

DEALING WITH FLARE-UPS

Many people will tell you that the way to deal with flare-ups is to have a squirt bottle of water handy to douse the offending flames. This is wrong. What happens when you do this is that you raise a plume of ash, which gets on the food you're cooking. Instead, when flare-ups occur—as they inevitably will when you are cooking any fatty food directly over the coals—simply move the food to the section of the grill with no coals, wait for the flare-up to die down, and then put the food back over the coals.

FLARE-UPS ARE CAUSED when fat drips on to the hot coals. Take away the cause of the problem by moving the food over to the "dead area" of the grill, and the flames quickly die down.

TAKE OUR ADVICE and cover the grill only when you're doing indirect-heat grilling, like barbecuing and smoke-roasting, where the food isn't directly over the coals.

BE PREPARED for emergencies; although you may never need it, having something on hand with which to douse the fire will give you peace of mind whenever you grill.

USING THE LID

Be sure you use the grill cover correctly. What this means—despite what most manufacturers tell you—is that you should cover the grill only when you are doing long, indirect cooking, never when you are cooking directly over the coals. When food is right over the coals, fat tends to drip into the fire, where it is transformed into rather acrid smoke. When the grill is uncovered, this smoke dissipates; with the grill covered, though, the food is bathed in that unpleasant smoke. It's not harmful, but it does give the food a distinct "off" flavor. When you are smoke-roasting, there is no fat dripping into the coals, and in any case the food spends long enough in contact with smoke from the charcoal to overcome any off flavor.

STAYING SAFE

Grilling is fun and you want to be relaxed when you're doing it, but you still need to pay attention to safety. After all, this is live fire. So always set up your grill on level ground in the largest possible open space, away from walls, fences, overhanging eaves or tree branches, or anything else that might easily catch fire. Never light a fire with gasoline, and never spray lighter fluid onto lit coals. We always have a fire extinguisher handy when we're grilling (although we keep it discreetly out of sight). If you don't have one, have a garden hose or bucket of sand nearby. Don't let kids or dogs run or play in the grilling area. And finally, always close down your grill, including the vents, after you are done with a grilling session.

KNOWING WHEN FOOD IS DONE

Since each live fire is a bit different from all others, the cooking times we give in recipes are really just estimates based on our experience. That means judging the doneness of food is perhaps the most important skill a grill cook can possess. Whichever method you use (*see opposite*), testing for yourself is of crucial importance, and we recommend that you do it early and often. Remember that there is only a relatively small window of perfect doneness, and you need to catch the food at that point.

IS IT DONE YET?

Whichever method you use to check for doneness, remember that the food will keep cooking for a while after it is removed from the heat (this is called "carryover cooking").

• Take that **steak** off when the degree of doneness is one less than you like it; when it looks rare if you really want it medium-rare, for example. The same goes for thick **chops** and juicy **roasts** of red meats.

• Remove **fish** from the flames when it still has a trace of translucency in the middle, since your ultimate aim is a fish (or **shrimp**) that is just barely opaque in the center.

• When it comes to **chicken**, though, ignore the rules above: Leave it on the fire until it is completely opaque all the way through and there is no pink at all in the center or, especially, down near the bone.

CARRYOVER COOKING Start checking for doneness well before you think the food is ready to come off the grill; it will continue to cook after it comes off the flames. If the recipe recommends letting meat rest, inverting a foil pan over it, or tenting it with aluminum foil, will keep it warm as it sits.

1. THE "HAND METHOD"

As protein cooks, it becomes increasingly firm. Experienced cooks can judge the degree of doneness of a piece of meat (or fowl or fish) simply by pushing on it with a finger. The firmer it is, the more done it is. Young cooks are taught that rare corresponds to the fleshy area (A) between the thumb and forefinger, for example, while well-done feels like the base of the thumb (B). This method does require a lot of practice. That doesn't mean it's not worth learning, it just means backing it up while you learn.

2. "NICK AND PEEK" METHOD

Totally practical, totally reliable: As the name implies, you simply pick up one of whatever you are cooking, nick it slightly with a knife so you can look inside, and check its state of doneness. That's all there is to it. You couldn't get much easier or more accurate. And don't worry about losing a lot of juice by cutting into the food; the very small amount of juice you may lose pales in comparison to serving raw or burned food.

3. A MEAT THERMOMETER

For large cuts of meat or whole fowl—basically anything that you grill-roast—the best option is to check the internal temperature. With a roast, you want to poke the thermometer all the way through to the other side of the meat, then draw it back to the midpoint to get a reading. When checking the doneness of a whole bird, insert the thermometer at an angle into the area between the drumstick and the breast, looking to hit the thickest part of the thigh.

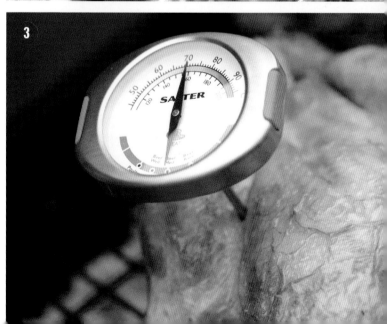

ENHANCING FLAVORS

The unique, supremely delicious taste of grilled food is a perfect vehicle for a wide range of flavor enhancers. From chiles, herbs, and spices used individually, to spice pastes and rubs to glazes and an astonishing variety of relishes, salsas, chutneys, sambals—not to mention traditional barbecue sauces—the grilling world is a world of deep flavor. And, of course, any grilled food is enhanced by the proper use of salt and pepper.

SALT

Add the right amount of salt to a dish, and all the other flavors open up, blend more harmoniously, and become fuller on the tongue. In other words, it tastes better. In our experience, most folks tend to use too little salt. Be a little more generous than you think you should, and you'll likely find your cooking improves. Our preference is for kosher rather than table salt. It has fewer additives, and its large crystals make it easier to judge just how much salt you're adding when you use your fingers—the best way to do it.

PEPPER

When it comes to pepper, there is no substitute for fresh ground, which has ten times the flavor of preground. We prefer to grind coarsely so the large chunks explode with flavor and heat in your mouth when you bite into them. As with salt, use it generously. For small amounts, a standard pepper grinder is fine. When you need more than a few tablespoons, you can either crack the peppercorns by rolling a heavy sauté pan back and forth over them while bearing down on the pan, or pulse them three or four times in a clean electric coffee grinder.

HERBS

The fresh, verdant flavors and aromaticity that herbs add to food can't be beat. We sometimes use the dried option when it is traditional in a certain type of dish, but are more likely to go for fresh herbs, since they are more vibrant. We particularly like to toss them into dishes at the end of cooking, an easy way of adding a spark of flavor. We're also very fond of the lovely Southeast Asian tradition of using fresh herbs as greens.

CHILES

Perhaps the most thrilling of all flavorings, chile peppers bring not only heat but also complex character to all kinds of dishes. However, their seemingly endless variety can be bewildering. If you're a true chile-head, then go ahead and experiment with every last one. Otherwise, we suggest you select a type that is readily available where you live, get to know it well, and feel free to use it anywhere we call for chiles in this book.

SPICES

Spices are a large part of what makes everyday food exciting. In fact, one of the things we like best about grilled food is that it has the character to stand up to the intensity of spices. If you can, it's best to buy spices whole and grind them yourself, which increases their depth of flavor exponentially. If you do buy spices preground, don't hold on to them too long, since their flavor fades markedly after a few months. We often toast spices—especially cumin and coriander—which gently brings out a whole new dimension of fragrance.

WHEN TO FLAVOR FOOD

We like to salt food before it goes on the fire. Some experts say you should avoid this because it draws moisture out of the food. But we think this is more than compensated for by the fact that the salt has a chance to interact with the food and amplify its flavors. When it comes to adding other flavorings before cooking, we prefer spice rubs and pastes to marinades because they give more intense flavor and can be used at the last minute. We also like to glaze food while it's on the grill—the sweet stickiness this imparts is especially suited to cuts of pork and poultry. And it's rare for us to grill without serving up a homemade accompaniment to the main dish—spicy or fragrant, fiery or cooling—so that our guests can help themselves to yet more flavor.

PREPARING YOUR OWN spice mixtures and relishes ensures that flavors are always super-fresh, clean, and lively.

A DRY SPICE MIXTURE can be bound together with olive oil or vegetable oil to form a paste that adheres well to food.

SPICE RUBS AND PASTES

The quickest and most effective way to add wonderfully intense flavors to grilled food is to coat it with a blend of spices before it goes on the grill. Whether dry (spice rubs) or wet (spice pastes), these mixtures work wonderfully well, since the high heat of the fire transforms them into hyper-flavorful crusts on the exterior of the food. Also, they can be made in advance, so all you have to do at the last minute is rub them on and you're ready to cook. Keep a supply of your favorite rub or mix handy, and you'll always be ready for a great grilled dinner.

AN ORDINARY PAINTBRUSH works better and lasts longer than a cook's pastry brush in the robust world of grilling.

TRADITIONAL CONDIMENTS such as mustard can be opened up by the addition of dried fruits such as apricots.

GLAZES

Who doesn't love food with a glistening, slightly sticky, sweetly flavorful glaze? Be careful, though, to add these flavorful coatings only during the last few minutes that the food is over the coals. Most glazes contain a sweetener—either in the form of sugar itself or in some other ingredient such as orange juice, honey, molasses, or currant jelly—so if you put the glaze on too early, these sugars will burn rather than properly caramelizing. As a bonus, surplus glaze mixture can be passed around as a sauce when you serve up the main dish.

ACCOMPANIMENTS

In traditional European cuisines, dishes are often accompanied with sauces created by deglazing what's left in the pan after the meat or fish is cooked. This is not possible with grilling, since there's no pan involved. But cooks in tropical climates, where grilling is the most common cooking method, have created a wide array of fruit and vegetable mixtures to accompany grilled food. Called by various names—salsas, chutneys, sambals, blatjangs, relishes—these inventive accompaniments bring a wealth of pungent, aromatic flavors to the table.

STEAKS, CHOPS, AND RIBS

FIRE AND MEAT WERE MADE FOR EACH OTHER.
AND HERE YOU'VE GOT IT ALL, FROM PRIMAL
STEAKS TO SUCCULENT RIBS—EVERY KIND OF RED
MEAT, WITH RUBS AND PASTES AND RELISHES
TO MAKE THEM EVEN MORE FLAVORFUL.
THIS IS WHAT GRILLING IS ALL ABOUT.

BLACK PEPPER-CRUSTED GRILLED RIBEYE WITH BLUE CHEESE-PECAN BUTTER

To us, the ribeye is the king of steaks, with the perfect combination of flavor and tenderness. A thick coating of freshly cracked black pepper, a little sprinkling of red pepper flakes, and a knob of butter enriched with blue cheese and toasted pecans is our favorite way of gilding this particular lily.

Serves 4

THE MEAT

½ cup freshly cracked black pepper
¼ cup kosher salt
1 tablespoon red pepper flakes
4 boneless ribeye steaks, about 1in (2.5cm) thick, 12–14oz (350–400g) each
2 tablespoons olive oil

THE BUTTER

1 tablespoon chopped pecans
¼ cup unsalted butter, softened
¼ cup crumbled blue cheese
1 teaspoon fresh lemon juice

Toast the pecans: Heat the oven to 350°F (180°C), spread the pecans over a shallow baking pan, and cook, checking frequently, until golden (5–10 minutes). Allow to cool.

Combine the butter, blue cheese, pecans, and lemon juice in a small bowl and mix well. Pile the butter mixture onto a piece of wax paper or plastic wrap, form it into a rough cylinder, and wrap it up. Refrigerate until firm. (This butter will keep in the refrigerator for a week, or frozen for several months.)

Build a fire in your grill. When the coals are all ignited, the flames have died down, and the temperature is hot (*see p34*), you're ready to cook.

Combine the black pepper, salt, and red pepper flakes in a small bowl and mix well. Rub the steaks all over with oil and coat generously with the spice mixture, pressing gently to be sure it adheres.

Put the steaks on the grill over the hottest part of the fire and cook, turning once, until very well seared—about 6–8 minutes per side for rare. To check for doneness, poke the steaks with your finger to test their firmness (*see p37*); if you're unsure, make a small cut in the thickest part of one steak to be sure it is just slightly less done than you like it.

While the steaks are cooking, cut the chilled blue cheese butter into ¼in (5mm) slices. As soon as the steaks come off the grill, top each steak with a slice or two of the butter, so it starts to melt as you serve the steaks.

CUBAN-STYLE SMOKED PORK RIBS
WITH MANGO MOJO

If you've ever traveled in the Latin Caribbean, you know that there are plenty of hardcore grillers down there, and they like to put a little different flavor profile on their ribs than we are used to up north. That's great with us, because we love the way lime, garlic, chiles, and sweet mango match up with the smoky ribs. This also works well using the oven-based "cheater" method found in our Memphis-style rib recipe (*see pp68–9*), since that lets you get a taste of the Caribbean even on days when you can't haul out the grill.

Serves 4 to 6

THE MEAT

¼ cup ground annatto (or substitute paprika)
2 tablespoons ground cumin
2 tablespoons kosher salt
2 tablespoons freshly cracked black pepper
2 tablespoons minced fresh garlic
2 racks pork spareribs, up to 3lb (1.35kg) each (known as 3.5/down in the trade)
2 tablespoons olive oil

THE MOJO

1 ripe mango, peeled, pitted, and diced small
½ cup olive oil
¼ cup distilled white vinegar
Juice of 2 limes (about ¼ cup)
¼ cup roughly chopped fresh cilantro
2 tablespoons minced fresh chile pepper of your choice
1 tablespoon minced fresh garlic
Kosher salt and freshly cracked black pepper to taste

Light a fire well over to one side of your grill, using enough coals to fill half a shoebox.

Combine the annatto, cumin, salt, pepper, and garlic in a small bowl and mix well. Rub the ribs with the oil, then coat them thoroughly on all sides with the spice mixture, pressing gently to be sure it adheres.

When the coals are well lit, place the ribs on the side of the grill away from the coals, being careful that none of the meat is directly over the coals. Put the lid on the grill with the vents open one-quarter of the way and cook, adding a handful of fresh charcoal about every 30 minutes, until the juice runs clear when you poke the meat with a fork and the meat is tender and pulls easily from the bone (3–4 hours).

While the ribs are cooking, combine the mojo ingredients in a small bowl, mix well, and set aside.

When the meat is done, remove from the grill, cut the racks into individual ribs, and serve "dry," passing the sauce on the side.

ROSEMARY-CRUSTED RACK OF LAMB
WITH OTHER GREEK FLAVORS

When we think of grilled lamb, we think of grilled peppers, and when we think of grilled peppers, we think of feta cheese. Here we put it all together by topping rib chops with a mix of grilled peppers, rosemary, feta, lemon, and parsley. You can cut the lamb racks into single chops for refined eaters, or double chops for a more robust meat experience.

Serves 4

THE MEAT

2 racks lamb, 12–14oz (350–400g) each
2 tablespoons vegetable oil
Kosher salt and freshly cracked black pepper to taste
3 tablespoons roughly chopped fresh rosemary

THE TOPPING

¼ cup extra virgin olive oil
Juice of 1 lemon (about ¼ cup)
¼ cup roughly chopped fresh parsley
4oz (115g) feta cheese, diced small or crumbled
Kosher salt and freshly cracked black pepper to taste
2 red, yellow, or orange bell peppers, halved lengthwise, cored, and seeded
1 tablespoon vegetable oil

Light a fire well over to one side of your grill, using enough coals to fill a large shoebox. When the fire has died down, the coals are covered in white ash, and the temperature is medium (*see p34*), you're ready to cook.

Rub the lamb racks with the vegetable oil, sprinkle them generously with salt and pepper, and pat all over with the rosemary, pressing gently to be sure it adheres.

Put the racks on the grill, fat side up, over the coals but near the edge of the fire. As soon as the side facing down is nicely browned, which should take about 15 minutes, flip the racks over and cook until the fat side is also well browned—about another 15 minutes. Watch carefully for flare-ups during this time; if they do occur, move the rack to the part of the grill with no coals until the flames have disappeared. To check for doneness, poke one of the racks with your finger to test its firmness (*see p37*); if you are unsure, insert a meat thermometer into the thickest part of the lamb, let it sit for 5 seconds, then read the temperature: look for 120°F (49°C) for rare, 126°F (52°C) for medium-rare (how we like it); 134°F (57°C) for medium, 150°F (65°C) for medium-well, and 160°F (71°C) for well done. When done to your liking, remove from the grill, cover loosely with foil, and allow to sit for 10 minutes.

While the lamb is cooking, combine the olive oil, lemon juice, and parsley in a small bowl, and whisk to blend. Add the feta cheese, season with salt and pepper, and set aside.

When the lamb is nearly done, rub the pepper halves with oil, season with salt and pepper, and grill directly over the coals until golden brown but still crisp (2–3 minutes per side). (Don't char them, since they won't be peeled.) When the peppers are done, cut them into ½in (1cm) wide strips, add to the bowl of feta, and toss gently.

Cut the lamb racks into double or single chops, arrange on a platter, and spoon the feta-pepper mixture over them.

LATIN-STYLE GRILLED PORK CHOPS
WITH PEACH-CHIPOTLE SALSA

We prefer spice rubs to marinades because they add more concentrated flavor, they can be put on at the last minute, and they encourage the formation of a nice crust on the outside of whatever you're putting on the grill. Here we rub pork chops with a simple Latin-style spice combination, and accompany them with a fresh salsa fueled by the chipotle, a chile that gets the relationship between heat and flavor just right. Try this one in late summer, when you want to add a little something extra to your pork chop repertoire, and peaches are at the height of their flavor.

Serves 4

THE MEAT

4 bone-in pork loin chops, about 12oz (350g) each, and 1in (2.5cm) thick
2 tablespoons olive oil

THE RUB

1 tablespoon ground cumin
1 tablespoon ground coriander
1 tablespoon chile powder
Kosher salt and freshly cracked black pepper to taste

THE SALSA

3 ripe but firm peaches, pitted and diced small
¼ cup red onion, diced small
1 tablespoon chipotle peppers in adobo sauce, mashed
Juice of 3 limes (about ⅓ cup)
⅓ cup roughly chopped fresh cilantro
Kosher salt and freshly cracked black pepper to taste

Build a fire in your grill. When the coals are all ignited, the flames have died down, and the temperature is medium (*see p34*), you're ready to cook.

While the fire is heating up, combine the ingredients for the spice rub in a small bowl and mix well. Rub the pork chops lightly with oil, then coat them generously with the spice rub. Set the chops aside while you make the salsa.

Make the salsa: Combine the peaches, onion, chipotle, lime juice, cilantro, and salt and pepper in a medium bowl and mix well. Set aside.

Put the chops on the grill over the coals and cook, turning once, until done to your liking (10–12 minutes per side for medium). To check for doneness, poke the meat with your finger to test its firmness (*see p37*); if you're unsure, cut into the thickest part of one of the chops and peek at the center to be sure it is just slightly less done than you like it.

Serve the chops hot, and pass the salsa on the side.

CUMIN-CRUSTED GRILLED SKIRT STEAK TACOS WITH ORANGE-CHILE GLAZE AND LIME-MARINATED AVOCADOS

Skirt steak has got to be one of the most underappreciated cuts of meat in the world. Not only is it incredibly easy to cook; its unique combination of leanness and fat makes it at once tender and flavorful, and it stacks up well against the strong tastes we love, like the Latin flavors that accompany it here. While chile powder will work just fine in the glaze, we recommend you seek out chipotles for their wonderful smoky heat.

Serves 4

THE MEAT

2½ lb (1 kg) trimmed skirt steak, cut into 4 pieces
1 large red onion, peeled and cut into ½ in (1 cm) thick rounds (keep rings together)
¼ cup olive oil
¼ cup cumin seeds
1 tablespoon paprika
Kosher salt and freshly cracked black pepper to taste

THE AVOCADOS

2 ripe but firm avocados
Juice of 6 limes (about ¾ cup)
¼ cup roughly chopped fresh cilantro
Kosher salt and freshly cracked black pepper to taste

THE GLAZE

1 cup fresh orange juice
½ cup distilled white vinegar
1 tablespoon tomato purée
1 tablespoon puréed chipotle chiles, or 1 tablespoon chile powder

THE WRAPS

12 corn tortillas, 6–8 in (15–20 cm) across

Combine the orange juice, vinegar, tomato purée, and chipotles or chile powder in a medium saucepan and, on the stove top, bring to a boil over high heat. Reduce the heat to medium and simmer vigorously until the mixture has reduced by two-thirds and become slightly syrupy (30–40 minutes). Remove the glaze from the heat and allow to cool to room temperature.

While the glaze reduces, halve, pit, and peel the avocados; cut each half into thin slices. Put the avocado slices, lime juice, and cilantro in a bowl, and sprinkle with salt and pepper. Toss gently until the avocado is evenly coated, then transfer to a serving dish, cover, and set aside until serving time.

Build a fire in your grill. When the coals are all ignited, the flames have died down, and the temperature is hot (*see p34*), you're ready to cook.

Rub the steaks and onion slices with olive oil and sprinkle evenly with the cumin, paprika, and salt and pepper.

When the fire is ready, put the steaks on the grill directly over the coals and cook until they are done to your liking (4–5 minutes per side for medium-rare). Brush the steaks generously with the glaze during the last 45 seconds of cooking on each side.

To check for doneness, poke each steak with your finger to test its firmness (*see p37*); if you're unsure, make a cut in the thickest part of one steak and peek at the center; it should be slightly less done than you like. Transfer the steaks to a cutting board, cover loosely with foil, and allow to rest for 5 minutes. Thinly slice the steak on the bias across the grain, arrange the slices on a serving platter, and drizzle with the remaining glaze.

While the steaks are resting, put the tortillas around the edges of the grill and cook briefly, flipping every 10 seconds or so, until they are soft and pliable (about 1 minute). Wrap the stack of warm tortillas in a large napkin or foil, and take them to the table along with the lime-marinated avocados and the steak, so your guests can "roll their own."

GRILLED VEAL CHOPS WITH GRILLED MUSHROOMS AND PORT

This elegant dish, rich with the deep, silky flavors of veal, mushrooms, butter, and port, is a great one for those times when you want to really pull out all the stops. Since veal is more delicate than beef you don't want to grill these chops as hard as you would a steak, but the smoky flavor that it gets over the coals still provides a great complement to the tender, subtle meat.

Serves 4

THE MEAT

4 veal rib chops, about 1½in (3.5cm) thick, 12–14oz (350–400g) each

2 tablespoons olive oil

2 tablespoons fresh thyme leaves

Kosher salt and freshly cracked black pepper to taste

THE MUSHROOMS

1lb (450g) white mushrooms, cleaned and stems trimmed

3 tablespoons olive oil

6 tablespoons unsalted butter

¼ cup port

¼ cup roughly chopped fresh parsley

Build a fire in your grill. When the coals are all ignited, the flames have died down, and the temperature is medium (*see p34*), you're ready to cook.

Rub the chops with the 2 tablespoons of olive oil, sprinkle the thyme over them, and season them generously with salt and pepper. Put them over the coals and grill until they are well seared on the outside and done to your liking inside (8–10 minutes per side for medium). To check for doneness, poke the chops with your finger to test the meat's firmness (*see p37*); if you're unsure, make a small cut and peek inside to be sure the chops are slightly less done than you like them, to allow for carryover cooking. When the chops are done, transfer them to a platter, cover them loosely with foil, and allow to rest for about 10 minutes.

While the chops are cooking, put the mushrooms and the 3 tablespoons of olive oil in a bowl and toss to coat. Put the mushrooms on the grill beside the chops and cook until they are moist all the way through (about 10 minutes). When the mushrooms are done, remove them from the grill, cut them into quarters, and return them to the bowl you tossed them in. Immediately add the butter, port, and parsley, and mix gently until the butter is melted and the mushrooms are evenly coated. Season with salt and pepper, and cover with foil to keep warm.

Put one chop on each plate, spoon some of the mushrooms on top, and serve.

SMOKED CURRIED BABY BACK RIBS
WITH INSANELY HOT SCOTCH BONNET SAUCE

The Scotch bonnet just might be our favorite chile pepper. Yes, it's very, very hot, but it's a heat backed up with intense, aromatic flavor. Here we match it with a spice rub that features curry powder, widely used in the West Indies where the Scotch bonnet originated. To shorten the cooking time, we use baby back ribs rather than the full-sized version. Beware—this dish is *really* hot.

Serves 4 to 6 as an appetizer

THE MEAT

¼ cup olive oil
¼ cup freshly cracked coriander seed
2 tablespoons curry powder
2 tablespoons paprika
1 tablespoon brown sugar
2 slabs baby back pork ribs, each about 1½lb (675g)

THE SAUCE

6–10 Scotch bonnet chiles, stemmed, but including seeds and ribs
⅓ cup fresh orange juice
⅓ cup cheap yellow mustard
¼ cup roughly chopped fresh cilantro
2 tablespoons dark brown sugar
Kosher salt and freshly cracked black pepper to taste

Light a fire well over to one side of your grill, using enough coals to fill half a shoebox.

Combine the olive oil, coriander, curry powder, paprika, and brown sugar in a small bowl and mix well. Rub this mixture all over the ribs.

When the flames have died down and the coals are covered in white ash, place the ribs on the side of the grill away from the coals, being careful that none of the meat is directly over the coals. Put the lid on the grill with the vents one-quarter of the way open. Cook the ribs for 30–45 minutes, adding a handful of fresh charcoal after 30 minutes. Turn the ribs over and cook them for 10–20 minutes more. To check for doneness, cut into one of the ribs to be sure that there is no pink down near the bone.

While the ribs are cooking, make the sauce: Combine the chiles, orange juice, mustard, cilantro, and brown sugar in a food processor or blender and purée.

When the ribs are done, brush them with the sauce and cook for about 30 seconds more on each side. Remove the ribs from the grill, cut them apart, and serve, passing any remaining sauce on the side.

INCENDIARY PORK TENDERLOINS
WITH GREEN CHILE-CORN SALSA

Along with Scotch bonnets, chipotles are our favorite chile peppers. Their unique, aromatic, smoky, pretty-much-indescribable flavor turns pork tenderloin into a spicy, flavorful luxury. We like chipotles in adobo sauce, although these days you can also find them dried. If you are using the dried ones, be sure to let them sit in boiling-hot water for about 20 minutes first, to plump up and become tender. The chile-corn salsa also goes great with just about any other pork dish, from a smoke-roasted loin to a plain grilled chop.

Serves 4

THE MEAT

2 pork tenderloins, about 1lb (450g) each
Kosher salt and freshly cracked black pepper to taste
½ cup roughly chopped chipotle peppers, preferably canned or jarred in adobo sauce (or substitute dried chipotles, soaked in hot water to reconstitute, and the Adobo Paste recipe on p189)

THE SALSA

2 smallish ears corn, husked and desilked
2–3 New Mexico or other hot green chiles of your choice, diced small
½ tomato about the size of a baseball, cored and diced small
Juice of 2 limes (about ¼ cup)
2 tablespoons roughly chopped fresh cilantro
1 teaspoon ground cumin
Kosher salt and freshly cracked black pepper to taste

Blanch the corn for the salsa: On the stove top, bring a large pan of salted water to a boil, and cook the ears for 1 minute. Drain, and when cool enough to handle, cut the kernels off the cobs.

Build a fire in your grill. When the coals are all ignited, the flames have died down, and the temperature is medium (*see p34*), you're ready to cook.

Sprinkle the tenderloins with salt and pepper, rub them all over with the chipotles and adobo sauce, and place them on the grill directly over the coals. Cook, rolling them around every 3–4 minutes to make sure they cook evenly, until they are done the way you like them (12–15 minutes for medium). To check for doneness, poke the meat with your finger to test its firmness (*see p37*); if you're unsure, cut into the pork at the thickest point to be sure it is slightly less done than you like. Transfer the tenderloins to a platter, cover loosely with foil, and allow to rest for 5–10 minutes.

While the pork is resting, combine the corn kernels with all of the other salsa ingredients in a bowl and mix well. Set aside.

Carve the pork tenderloins crosswise into ½in (1cm) thick slices and arrange them on a serving platter. Spoon the salsa over the pork and serve, passing any remaining salsa separately.

ROSEMARY-GRILLED NEW YORK STRIP
STEAK WITH CARAMELIZED RED ONION JAM

Steak on the grill is the ultimate classic, and for good reason: The rich, deep flavor of beef is perhaps the ideal foil for the smoky char of the grill. This simple, straightforward recipe adds a little aromatic rosemary and garlic to the mix, along with an easy but flavorful onion jam. The jam will last for 10 days, covered and refrigerated, so you might want to make a double batch during high grilling season; it's great with pork and hamburgers as well as steak.

Serves 4

THE MEAT

3 tablespoons roughly chopped fresh rosemary
3 tablespoons olive oil
1 garlic clove, peeled
1 tablespoon kosher salt
1 tablespoon freshly cracked black pepper
4 boneless loin shell steaks, about 1½in (3–4cm) thick, 12–14oz (350–400g) each

THE ONION JAM

1 head garlic
3 tablespoons olive oil, divided
2 medium red onions, peeled and thinly sliced
Kosher salt and freshly cracked black pepper to taste
¼ cup balsamic vinegar
1 tablespoon dark brown sugar

For the jam: Heat the oven to 300°F (150°C); slice the top quarter off the head of garlic, set it on a sheet of foil and sprinkle with one tablespoon of the olive oil, salt, and pepper, then wrap and braise until soft (about 1 hour). Set it aside to cool. On the stove top, heat the rest of the olive oil in a large sauté pan or skillet over medium heat until it is hot but not smoking. Add the onions, sprinkle with salt and pepper, and sauté until the onions start to soften (about 5 minutes). Reduce the heat to low and continue to cook, stirring often, until the onions are well caramelized (20–30 minutes). Making sure the garlic is cool enough to handle, squeeze the flesh from each clove. Add the garlic to the onions, stirring to incorporate, then add the vinegar and brown sugar and mix well. Continue cooking until the mixture is sticky and thickens slightly (about 2 minutes more). Remove from the heat and set aside.

While the onions are cooking, build a multilevel fire in your grill (*see p31*). When the coals are all ignited, the flames have died down, and the temperature is hot (*see p34*), you're ready to cook.

Combine the rosemary, olive oil, garlic clove, and salt and pepper in a mortar and pestle or small, sturdy bowl and mash to a paste. Dry the steaks with paper towels, and rub them all over with the seasoning paste. Put the steaks on the grill over the hottest coals and sear them well (4–5 minutes per side). Slide the steaks over to the cooler part of the grill and continue to cook, turning once, until they are done to your liking (10–12 minutes more for rare). To check for doneness, poke the steaks with your finger to test their firmness (*see p37*); if you're unsure, make a small cut in the thickest steak—it should be just slightly less done than you like it. Transfer the steaks to a serving platter and cover loosely with foil. Let them rest for 5–10 minutes before serving with the onion jam.

FLAVOR FOOTPRINT MEXICAN-LATIN

A prime characteristic of Mexican cooking is the expert and varied use of a huge range of chiles, both fresh and dried. This distinguishes it from many other Latin American cuisines, which are not particularly spicy. But most do share a reliance on the herbs cilantro (or *culantro,* a local variant) and oregano, the spices cumin and bay, the juice of oranges and limes, and large quantities of garlic, among other ingredients. If you're unfamiliar with the dynamic cuisines of Latin America, the complex flavors of these simple combinations are going to bring you very pleasant surprises.

All-Purpose Latin Spice Rub
Makes about 1 cup

The name says it all—you can rub this on just about anything that you are going to put on the grill. Use a mortar and pestle or the base of a heavy skillet to crack the coriander seeds.

½ cup freshly cracked coriander seeds
⅓ cup cumin seeds
2 tablespoons freshly cracked black pepper
1 tablespoon kosher salt

Combine all the ingredients in a small bowl and mix well. Stored in an airtight container and kept in a cool, dark place, this dry rub will last for a month or longer.

Ancho Chile Paste
Makes about ¾ cup

Rub this onto beef or pork just before it goes on the grill, or use it as a kind of quick marinade and let the flavors soak in and combine for up to 4 hours.

¼ cup ancho chiles
¼ cup roughly chopped fresh cilantro
¼ cup olive oil
2 tablespoons cumin seeds
Juice of 1 lime (about 2 tablespoons)
1 tablespoon minced fresh garlic
1 tablespoon kosher salt
1 tablespoon freshly cracked black pepper

Soak the chiles in enough hot water to cover them for 20 minutes to rehydrate, then drain and combine with all the other ingredients. Purée in a food processor, or use a pestle and mortar to mash to a paste. This paste will keep, covered and refrigerated, for 2–3 days.

Ancho Chile Paste

Quick Salsa Rojo
Makes about 2 cups

This classic red salsa is very versatile; it goes beautifully with just about any grilled food.

2 ripe tomatoes, cored and diced small (about 1½ cups)
½ small red onion, peeled and diced (about ⅓ cup)
¼ cup roughly chopped fresh cilantro
Juice of 2 limes (about ¼ cup)
1 tablespoon chopped fresh green chile pepper of your choice
1 teaspoon ground cumin
Kosher salt and freshly cracked black pepper to taste

Combine all the ingredients in a medium-sized bowl and mix well. This is best used the day it is made, but will keep, covered and refrigerated, for 3–4 days.

Molasses-Jalapeño Barbecue Sauce
Makes about 2 cups

This simple sauce makes a perfect last-minute glaze or accompanying dipping sauce for all manner of grilled food.

1 cup ketchup
⅓ cup molasses
Juice of 3 limes (about ⅓ cup)
⅓ cup roughly chopped fresh cilantro
3 tablespoons chopped jalapeño or other fresh green chile pepper of your choice
Kosher salt and freshly cracked black pepper to taste

Combine all the ingredients in a medium-sized bowl and mix well. This sauce will keep, covered and refrigerated, for 3–4 days.

SIGNATURE INGREDIENTS/TOP ROW (LEFT TO RIGHT) Fresh chiles, dried chiles, cilantro; **SECOND ROW** Coriander, lime, oregano; **THIRD ROW** Avocado, annatto seeds, garlic; **BOTTOM ROW** Cumin, bay leaves, orange.

Green Apple-Chipotle Salsa
Makes about 1½ cups

We always like to use green apples in Latin salsas. Their crunch and freshness remind us of jicama, a favorite vegetable of Chris's that holds its juicy, crisp texture beautifully when chopped into salads. This chunky combo is best as an accompaniment to pork, fish, or chicken.

2 Granny Smith apples, cored and diced small
½ red onion, peeled and diced small
2 tablespoons minced chipotle peppers in adobo sauce
Juice of 1 lime (about 2 tablespoons)
2 tablespoons roughly chopped fresh cilantro
1 teaspoon ground cumin
Kosher salt and freshly cracked black pepper to taste

Combine all the ingredients in a medium-sized bowl and mix well. This salsa is best served right away, but will keep, covered and refrigerated, for 2–3 days.

Green Apple-Chipotle Salsa

WHITE PEPPER-CRUSTED GRILLED FLANK STEAK WITH MAPLE-SOY GLAZE

Although we're generally not in favor of "fusion" cooking, occasionally there's some unlikely combination of ingredients that works so well it's worth it. Here's one such instance—the earthy sweetness of the quintessentially American maple syrup works perfectly with a collection of Asian flavors, from salty soy sauce to aromatic sesame oil and ginger. This is a great dish for those times when you want a quick dinner that's anything but routine.

Serves 4

THE MEAT

¼ cup freshly cracked white pepper
2 tablespoons Asian sesame oil
2 tablespoons soy sauce
1 tablespoon peeled and minced fresh ginger
Kosher salt to taste
1 flank steak, about 2lb (900g)
¼ cup roughly chopped scallions with green tops

THE GLAZE

⅓ cup maple syrup (grade B if possible)
¼ cup soy sauce
2 tablespoons Asian sesame oil
1 tablespoon peeled and minced fresh ginger
½ cup chopped scallions (white and green parts)
1 teaspoon red pepper flakes

Build a fire in your grill. When the coals are all ignited, the flames have died down, and the temperature is hot (*see p34*), you're ready to cook.

Combine all the glaze ingredients in a small bowl, mix well, and set aside.

Combine the white pepper, sesame oil, soy sauce, ginger, and salt in another small bowl. Rub this mixture all over the flank steak. Place the steak over the coals, and grill for 5–7 minutes per side for medium-rare, depending on thickness; brush with glaze during the last minute of cooking on each side. To check for doneness, poke the steak with your finger to test its firmness (*see p37*); if you're unsure, make a small cut and peek inside to be sure that it is slightly less done than you like it, to allow for carryover cooking. Set the steak aside to rest for about 10 minutes before carving.

Slice the steak thinly on the bias across the grain. Arrange the slices on a serving platter, drizzle with some of the glaze, and sprinkle with scallions. Pass any remaining glaze on the side.

GRILLED KOREAN-STYLE SHORT RIBS
WITH CHILE SLAW

Grilling short ribs, which is traditional in Korea, is an unusual approach to a cut of meat that's usually braised. It works beautifully, but be sure you use good-quality meat here; gnarly ribs are going to be tough cooked this way, even after marinating. The chile slaw makes a great accompaniment to any kind of grilled beef, so long as you're a heat-lover.

Serves 4

THE MEAT

3lb (1.35kg) flanken-style beef short ribs,
　½in (1cm) thick

THE SLAW

¼ cup rice wine vinegar
¼ cup Southeast Asian chile-garlic sauce
1 tablespoon granulated sugar
1 tablespoon peeled and minced fresh ginger
2 cups shredded Napa cabbage

THE MARINADE

¼ cup soy sauce
2 tablespoons Asian sesame oil
2 tablespoons distilled white vinegar
2 tablespoons chopped fresh chile pepper of your choice
2 tablespoons red pepper flakes
2 tablespoons peeled and minced fresh ginger
1 tablespoon minced fresh garlic
1 teaspoon granulated sugar
Kosher salt and freshly cracked black pepper to taste

Place the short ribs in a large bowl. Combine the marinade ingredients in a small bowl and mix well, then pour the mixture over the ribs, turning them to coat. Cover and refrigerate for about 2 hours, turning once or twice.

Meanwhile, combine the vinegar, chile-garlic sauce, sugar, and ginger in a small bowl and mix well. Put the cabbage in a large bowl and pour just enough of the dressing over it to moisten, tossing to coat. Cover and refrigerate until serving time.

Build a fire in your grill. When the coals are all ignited, the flames have died down, and the temperature is very hot (*see p34*), you're ready to cook.

Remove the meat from the marinade and pat it dry with paper towels. (Reserve the marinade.) Place the ribs on the grill and cook until they are well seared on one side (about 3 minutes). Turn and continue cooking to the desired doneness—about 3 minutes more for rare—basting with the reserved marinade during the last minute of cooking. To check for doneness, cut into the meat near a bone to be sure it is slightly less done than you like.

When the ribs are done, transfer them to a serving platter, cover loosely with foil, and allow to rest for 5 minutes. Cut the meat between the bones into individual ribs, and serve them hot, accompanied by the chile slaw.

EASY MEMPHIS-STYLE BARBECUED PORK SPARERIBS

This is for those of you who don't have the patience or the space to make slow-barbecued ribs. Although they only spend a few minutes on the grill (after several hours in the oven), this version is still mighty delicious. In fact, once they're oven-cooked, you can refrigerate them for up to two days before finishing them off on the grill. They are "Memphis-style" because, like the pitmasters of that rib-centric city, we don't put sauce on the meat. Instead, we coat them with our Traditional Barbecue Rub before they get cooked, then pass the sauce separately along with the cooked ribs. That way, the ribs have a nice, crisp, dry crust on the outside, which you can coat with as much sauce as you like.

Serves 4 to 6

THE MEAT

2 racks pork spareribs, up to 3lb (1.35kg) each

THE SAUCE

1 cup ketchup
⅓ cup cider vinegar
¼ cup brown sugar
¼ cup orange juice
2 tablespoons prepared brown mustard
½ teaspoon "liquid smoke" (optional)
Kosher salt and freshly cracked black pepper to taste

TRADITIONAL BARBECUE RUB

⅓ cup kosher salt
⅓ cup freshly cracked black pepper
¼ cup dark brown sugar
2 tablespoons ground paprika
2 tablespoons ground chile powder
2 tablespoons ground cumin
2 tablespoons ground coriander
2 tablespoons ground cayenne pepper
1 tablespoon ground ginger

In a small bowl, combine all the rub ingredients and mix well. (If you want to multiply the quantities, this mixture will keep, covered and stored in a cool, dry place, for months; it's great with any pork cut or with chicken.)

Preheat the oven to 200°F (95°C). Coat the ribs thoroughly with the barbecue rub, set them on baking sheets, and roast until the meat is tender and pulls easily from the bone (about 3 hours). Remove the ribs from the oven.

While the ribs are cooking, combine the sauce ingredients in a small bowl, mix well, and set aside.

When the ribs are nearly done, light a small fire in your grill. You want a very low charcoal fire with the grill rack set as high as possible. When the ribs are done, put them on the grill for as long as your patience allows—at least until a light crust has formed, which can take from 10 to 20 minutes per side, depending on your fire. Of course, the longer the ribs cook, the better. Brush them with sauce during the last minute of cooking.

Cut the racks into individual ribs and serve, passing the remaining sauce on the side.

SOUTHWESTERN GRILLED LAMB SHOULDER CHOPS WITH SPICY GRILLED AVOCADOS

We are big fans of lamb shoulder chops. Although less tender than the more commonly used rib chops, they have deeper lamb flavor and are much less expensive. They are also robust enough to stand up to the dynamic Southwestern flavors we pair them with here. And, if you have never had grilled avocados before, you are in for a big treat.

Serves 4

THE MEAT

8 lamb shoulder chops, about 6oz (175g) each
2 tablespoons olive oil
2 tablespoons ground cumin
1 tablespoon minced fresh garlic
Kosher salt and freshly cracked black pepper to taste

THE AVOCADOS

2 ripe avocados, halved and pitted
2 tablespoons olive oil
2 tablespoons chile powder
Kosher salt and freshly cracked black pepper to taste

THE VINAIGRETTE

½ cup olive oil
Juice of 2 limes (about ¼ cup)
3 tablespoons chopped fresh cilantro
2 tablespoons minced chipotle peppers in adobo sauce
1 tablespoon prepared brown mustard
1 teaspoon minced fresh garlic
Kosher salt and freshly cracked black pepper to taste

Build a fire in your grill. When the coals are all ignited, the flames have died down, and the temperature is medium-hot (*see p34*), you're ready to cook.

Combine all the vinaigrette ingredients in a small bowl, mix well, and set aside.

Rub the chops lightly with the olive oil, then rub them all over with the cumin, sprinkle them with the garlic, and season generously with salt and pepper. Place on the grill and cook until they are done to your liking (4–5 minutes per side for medium-rare). To check for doneness, poke the chops with your finger to test their firmness (*see p37*); if you're unsure, make a small cut in one chop to be sure that it is slightly less done than you like it. When the chops are done, transfer them to a platter, cover loosely with foil, and allow them to rest for about 10 minutes.

While the chops are resting, rub the cut sides of the avocado halves with oil and sprinkle them generously with chile powder and salt and pepper. Place them cut side down on the grill and cook until they are golden brown and slightly charred (3–5 minutes). Arrange the cooked avocados cut side up around the chops on the platter. Stir the vinaigrette to blend and drizzle it generously over everything.

ARGENTINA: IN THE LAND OF BEEF

Driving back to Buenos Aires after a few days out in the immense grasslands known as the pampas, we spied the telltale sign: racks of meat splayed out on a metal stand slanted over a smoldering wood fire.

Braking our little power-deprived car, we swerved into the driveway of the shed behind the fire pit, noting with approval that the restaurant had no name, just a sign outside that said "Domingo-Asado"—"Sunday-Barbecue." Everybody has heard that Argentina is all about beef, but until you see it for yourself, it's hard to believe. On every street corner in every city, it seems, you'll find a *parillada* serving delicious grass-fed beef, most at bargain prices. But the apotheosis of the Argentine beef experience is the *asado*, a cultural ritual born on the pampas. There the cowboys known as gauchos developed a celebratory event in which they slaughtered a cow in the morning, then slowly cooked every bit of it over a wood fire, eating the various cuts as they were done. Like barbecue in the American South or cassoulet in Provence, *asado* is more than just a dish; it is a badge of cultural identity. And the meal we ate in that little shed outside Buenos Aires still followed the formalized sequence: First came a platter of "organ meats"—rich sweetbreads, slightly chewy intestines, fatty chorizo sausage, thick blood sausages—with the obligatory bowl of *chimichurri* sauce. Then, along with a bottle of Malbec wine, a platter of more substantial fare: Short ribs, skirt steak, and what the French call entrecôte. At this point we were sated, but we bravely tackled the final wooden platter, this one bearing a giant T-bone and a slab of rump steak. We practically crawled away from the table, but we were satisfied that we had experienced the heart of Argentine cooking.

GRILLED GIANT T-BONE STEAKS
WITH PARSLEY SAUCE

The classic American steak, T-bone combines a bit of the tenderloin and a bit of the loin. Complementing its full, beefy flavor is a sauce inspired by the *chimichurri* that is a table staple in Argentina and Uruguay, those bastions of beef. The sauce's combination of heat, acidity, and herbaceousness sets up the meat perfectly without overwhelming it. This dish has become a mainstay of Saturday nights at the East Coast Grill, when Executive Chef Eric Gburski breaks out the awesome steaks.

Serves 4

2 large (at least 24oz/700g) T-bone steaks, each 1½in (3–4cm) thick
2 tablespoons olive oil
⅓ cup freshly cracked black pepper
¼ cup kosher salt

For the sauce:
⅓ cup roughly chopped fresh parsley leaves
½ small red onion, peeled and finely chopped (about ¼ cup)
⅓ cup extra virgin olive oil
Juice of 1 lemon (about ¼ cup)
¼ cup balsamic vinegar
2 teaspoons red pepper flakes (optional)
Kosher salt and freshly cracked black pepper to taste

Build a multilevel fire (*see p31*) in your grill. When the coals are all ignited, the flames have died down, and the temperature is hot (*see p34*), you're ready to cook.

Rub the steaks all over with oil and coat them generously with pepper and salt, pressing gently to be sure it adheres.

Put the steaks on the grill over the hottest part of the fire and cook, turning once, until well seared (6–8 minutes per side). Move the steaks to the cooler side of the grill, cover them with a metal pie pan or disposable foil pan, and let them cook slowly until they are done to your liking (8–10 minutes more per side for rare). To check for doneness, poke the steaks with your finger to test their firmness (*see p37*); if you're unsure, make a small cut in the thickest part of one steak to be sure it is just slightly less done inside than you like it.

While the steaks are cooking, combine the sauce ingredients in a bowl and whisk until well blended.

When the steaks are ready, carve them into thick strips, arrange them on a serving platter, drizzle generously with the sauce, and pass the remaining sauce on the side.

GRILLED LAMB SIRLOIN MEDALLIONS
WITH ROASTED PEPPER AND BLACK OLIVE RELISH

Lamb top sirloin is a great cut of meat, tender but with plenty of lamb flavor. Here we cut it into medallions, sprinkle it with coriander and fennel seeds to accent its slightly aromatic nature, and put it over the coals for just a few minutes. Served with a rather earthy, slightly sharp relish, it's one of our new favorite lamb dishes. If you already have a fire going, you can grill fresh red peppers for the relish (*for method see p78*), but using jarred ones from the pantry makes this a really fast and simple dish to prepare.

Serves 4

THE MEAT

¼ cup freshly cracked black pepper

¼ cup kosher salt

1 tablespoon coriander seeds, freshly cracked

1 tablespoon fennel seeds, freshly cracked

2 lamb top sirloins, 16–18oz (450–500g) each, cut into 1in (2.5cm) thick medallions

2 tablespoons olive oil

THE RELISH

1 cup diced roasted red peppers, jarred or homemade

⅓ cup brine-cured black olives, such as kalamata, pitted and roughly chopped

¼ cup roughly chopped fresh basil

¼ cup extra virgin olive oil

¼ cup balsamic vinegar

1 tablespoon minced fresh garlic

Kosher salt and freshly cracked black pepper to taste

Build a fire in your grill. When the coals are all ignited, the flames have died down, and the temperature is medium-hot (*see p34*), you're ready to cook.

Combine the relish ingredients in a small bowl and mix well.

Combine the black pepper, salt, coriander, and fennel in a small bowl and mix well. Rub the lamb with oil and coat it generously with the spice mixture, pressing gently to be sure it adheres. Put the medallions on the grill directly over the coals and cook until they are slightly less done than you like them (6–8 minutes per side for rare). To check for doneness, press the meat with your finger to test its firmness (*see p37*), or make a cut into one medallion and peek inside to check that it is slightly less done than you like it.

Arrange the medallions on a platter, top each with a spoonful of relish, and pass the remaining relish on the side.

GRILLED LAMB CHOPS WITH ROASTED RED PEPPER-WALNUT RELISH

The incredible aroma of lamb cooking over an open fire always has two effects on us: It evokes memories of those parts of the world where lamb is king, particularly North Africa, Greece, and Turkey; and it makes us very hungry. The relish that accompanies the lamb chops here—rich with roasted peppers and nuts, with the aroma of mint and the sweet-tart bite of pomegranate molasses—is our homage to the Turkish classic *muhammara*. Although there is truly no substitute for pomegranate molasses, if you can't find it you can use equal parts regular molasses and lemon juice.

Serves 4

THE MEAT

8 lamb loin chops, about 6oz (175g) each, and 1½in (3.5cm) thick
2 tablespoons olive oil
1 teaspoon ground fennel seed
Kosher salt and freshly cracked black pepper to taste

THE RELISH

⅓ cup walnuts
3 red bell peppers
2 tablespoons extra virgin olive oil
¼ cup roughly chopped fresh mint
2 tablespoons pomegranate molasses
1 teaspoon minced garlic
Kosher salt and freshly cracked black pepper to taste

Toast the walnuts: Heat the oven to 350°F (180°C), spread the nuts over a shallow baking pan, and cook, checking frequently, until golden (5–10 minutes). Allow to cool, then roughly chop them.

Build a multilevel fire in your grill (*see p31*). When the coals are all ignited, the flames have died down, and the temperature is hot (*see p34*), you're ready to cook.

Put the bell peppers on the hot side of the grill and cook, rolling them around, until the skins are completely black and blistered on all sides (8–12 minutes). Put them in a paper bag, fold it closed, and set aside until the peppers are cool enough to handle. Then gently pull the skin from the peppers, tear them open, remove the seeds, ribs, and stem, and dice them medium.

Rub the chops with the oil and sprinkle with the fennel, salt, and pepper. Place the chops on the hot side of the grill and sear well, about 6 minutes per side. Move the chops to the cooler side of the grill and cook, turning once, until done as you like (4–6 minutes more for rare). To check for doneness, make a cut in the thickest part of one chop and peek inside; it should be slightly less done than you like it. Remove the chops from the grill, cover them loosely with foil, and allow to rest for 5 minutes.

While the chops are cooking, combine all the relish ingredients in a medium bowl and mix well.

Put a generous spoonful of relish on each of four dishes, top with a chop, and pass the remaining relish on the side.

MEDITERRANEAN SPICE-RUBBED PORK CHOPS WITH APRICOT-MINT RELISH

Spices from the Mediterranean make these pork chops taste at once familiar and slightly exotic; you could serve them twice a week without seeming too "out there" or boring your taste buds. An apricot relish brings freshness and a bit of heat to the party. This recipe makes more spice rub than you need, but it keeps well, and is great on lamb or chicken too.

Serves 4

THE MEAT

4 pork rib chops, about 1½in (3.5cm) thick, 12–14oz (350–400g) each
2 tablespoons olive oil

THE RELISH

3 ripe apricots, pitted and diced medium (about 1 cup)
¼ cup roughly chopped fresh mint
Juice of ½ lemon (about 2 tablespoons)
4 dashes Tabasco sauce
Kosher salt and freshly cracked black pepper to taste

THE SPICE RUB

¼ cup sesame seeds
⅓ cup coriander seeds, freshly cracked
2 tablespoons ground fenugreek
2 tablespoons dried oregano
1 tablespoon ground cumin
1 tablespoon kosher salt
Pinch ground cinnamon

Build a multilevel fire in your grill (*see p31*). When the coals are all ignited, the flames have died down, and the temperature is medium (*see p34*), you're ready to cook.

For the spice rub, toast the sesame seeds in a dry skillet on the grill, shaking them frequently to prevent burning, until they become just a shade darker (3–5 minutes).

Combine the spice rub ingredients in a small bowl and mix well. Measure out about ¼ cup of the rub for the pork chops. Rub the chops with oil and coat them with the spice rub, pressing gently to be sure it adheres.

Put the chops on the grill over the hotter part of the fire and cook, turning once, until well seared (3–4 minutes per side). Move the chops to the cooler side of the grill, cover them with a metal pie pan or disposable foil pan, and let them cook slowly until they are done to your liking (8–10 minutes per side for medium). To check for doneness, poke the chops with your finger to test their firmness (*see p37*); if you're unsure, make a small cut in the thickest part of one chop to be sure it is just slightly less done than you like it.

While the chops are on the grill, combine the apricots, mint, lemon juice, Tabasco, and salt and pepper in a small bowl and mix well. Transfer to a serving dish and set aside.

Transfer the chops to a platter and serve, passing the relish on the side.

MOLASSES & CHILE-GLAZED PORK MEDALLIONS WITH SMOKY CORN-RED PEPPER RELISH

If you make this dish with pork raised in the old-fashioned way so it has plenty of fat and flavor, it's going to be out of this world; but it is still fantastic even with today's leaner pork, because it has so many wonderful flavors going on in the glaze and the relish. If you have any relish left over, try it with simple grilled fish, or in any cold meat sandwich.

Serves 4

THE MEAT

⅓ cup molasses
2 tablespoons butter, melted
1 tablespoon red pepper flakes
1 tablespoon freshly cracked black pepper
8 pork loin cutlets, ¾ in (2cm) thick, 5oz (140g) each
2 tablespoons olive oil
Kosher salt and freshly cracked black pepper

THE RELISH

1 red pepper
3 ears corn, shucked and de-silked
¼ cup roughly chopped fresh basil
3 tablespoons extra virgin olive oil
3 tablespoons balsamic vinegar
1 teaspoon minced fresh garlic
Kosher salt and freshly cracked black pepper to taste

Build a fire in your grill. When the coals are all ignited, the flames have died down, and the temperature is medium-hot (*see p34*), you're ready to cook.

For the relish, put the pepper on the grill, rolling it around until the skin is completely black and blistered on all sides (8–12 minutes). Put it in a paper bag, fold it closed, and set aside until the pepper is cool enough to handle. Then gently pull the skin from the pepper, tear it open, remove the seeds, ribs, and stem, and dice medium. While the pepper is cooling, put the ears of corn on the grill over the coals and cook, rolling them around occasionally, until they are starting to brown and are a little bit tender (3–4 minutes). Transfer the ears to a cutting board and slice the kernels off the cobs; you should have about 1½ cups of kernels. Combine the roasted red pepper, toasted corn, basil, oil, vinegar, and garlic in a medium bowl and mix well. Season to taste with salt and pepper, then transfer the relish to a serving dish.

Make the glaze: Combine the molasses, butter, red pepper flakes, and pepper in a small bowl and mix well.

Dry the pork cutlets with paper towels, rub them all over with olive oil, and sprinkle them generously with salt and pepper. Put them on the grill directly over the coals and cook, turning once, until done to your liking (about 5 minutes per side for medium-well done). Brush them with the glaze during the last 30 seconds of cooking on each side. To check for doneness, poke the meat with your finger to test its firmness (*see p37*). If you're unsure, make a small cut in it; it should be just slightly less done than you like it. Transfer the cutlets to a serving platter, cover them loosely with foil, and let them rest for 5 minutes before serving with the relish and any remaining glaze.

GRILLED COWBOY STEAK WITH BARBECUED LEEKS AND WHOLEGRAIN APRICOT MUSTARD

We love bone-in ribeye steaks—they are right up there on the tenderness scale, but because they are well-marbled they also have plenty of deep, beefy flavor. To accompany them, leeks make a nice change from the standard grilled onions, and in place of horseradish, we give you a super-quick way to perk up store-bought wholegrain mustard.

Serves 2

THE MEAT

1 tablespoon ground cumin
1 tablespoon ground coriander
1 tablespoon chile powder
2 tablespoons kosher salt
¼ cup freshly cracked black pepper
1 bone-in ribeye steak, about 2lb (900g) and 2in (5cm) thick
2 tablespoons olive oil

THE LEEKS

4 leeks, white parts only, trimmed and very well washed
1 tablespoon olive oil

THE MUSTARD

¼ cup wholegrain mustard
2 tablespoons finely chopped dried apricot

Build a multilevel fire in your grill (see p31). When the coals are all ignited, the flames have died down, and the temperature is hot (see p34), you're ready to cook.

Combine the cumin, coriander, chile powder, salt, and pepper in a small bowl and mix well.

Rub the steak with some of the oil, then sprinkle it with about two-thirds of the spice mixture, pressing down gently to be sure it adheres. Put the steak on the grill directly over the hottest part of the fire and sear very well for 5–8 minutes per side, then move to the cooler part of the grill and continue to cook until it is done to your liking (8–10 minutes more per side for rare). To check for doneness, poke the meat with your finger to test its firmness (see p37). If you're unsure, make a cut into the center; it should be just slightly less done than you like it. Remove from the grill, cover loosely with foil, and allow to rest for 5 minutes.

While the steak is searing, rub the leeks with the remaining oil and sprinkle with the remaining spice rub. When you move the steak to the cooler side of the grill, lay the leeks beside it and cook them, rolling around occasionally for even cooking, until they are golden brown and slightly charred (8–12 minutes). Transfer the leeks to a cutting board, halve them lengthwise, then slice crosswise into half-moons about ½in (1cm) wide. Cover to keep warm until the steak is done.

Mix the mustard and the apricots together until evenly combined.

Transfer the steak to a platter (halved or sliced as you wish) and arrange the leeks, cut side up, around the meat. Dab both with the apricot mustard and serve, passing additional mustard on the side.

GRILLED FILET MIGNON WITH GORGONZOLA, PANCETTA, AND PEACH-BALSAMIC JAM

Got a special occasion coming up? Looking for the most sumptuous steak dinner possible? Look no further. There's a reason that filet mignon is a byword for steak luxury —it's the single most tender cut of beef, with a meltingly smooth texture. In this Italian-influenced spin on the classic trio of steak, blue cheese, and bacon, we top the steak with a little slab of Gorgonzola cheese and scatter pancetta over the top. For the final touch, we add a fresh peach jam with Italian flavors. Now, that's a celebration.

Serves 4

THE STEAKS

8oz (225g) pancetta, diced small (or substitute bacon)
4 beef filet steaks, 8–10oz (225–280g) each, about 2in (5cm) thick
2 tablespoons olive oil
Kosher salt and freshly cracked black pepper to taste
4 slices Gorgonzola, about 2oz (60g) each

THE JAM

2 tablespoons olive oil
1 medium red onion, peeled and diced small
3 ripe but firm peaches, pitted and diced medium
⅓ cup balsamic vinegar
⅓ cup freshly squeezed orange juice
1 tablespoon dark brown sugar
Kosher salt and freshly cracked black pepper to taste

Make the jam: On the stove top, heat the olive oil in a large sauté pan over medium-high heat until hot but not smoking. Add the onion and cook, stirring occasionally, until translucent (7–9 minutes). Add the peaches and cook, stirring frequently, for another 3 minutes—you just want the peaches to be nicely softened. Add the vinegar, orange juice, brown sugar, and salt and pepper and bring to a boil. Reduce the heat to medium-low and simmer until the jam begins to thicken (8–10 minutes). Remove from the heat and set aside.

Build a multilevel fire in your grill (*see p31*). When the coals are all ignited, the flames have died down, and the temperature is hot (*see p34*), you're ready to cook.

While the fire heats up, sauté the pancetta on the stove top over medium-low heat, turning frequently until it is crisp and brown—about 7 minutes. Transfer to paper towels to drain, then to a small bowl; cover to keep warm.

Rub the steaks with oil and sprinkle generously with salt and pepper. When the grill is ready, put the steaks over the hottest coals and sear well for 6–8 minutes per side. Move the steaks to the cooler part of the fire, cover with a pie plate or disposable foil pan, and cook for another 8–10 minutes, until done to your liking. To check for doneness, poke the meat with your finger to test its firmness (*see p37*); if you're unsure, cut into it and look to be sure it is just slightly less done than you like it.

Transfer the steaks to a serving platter and top with the cheese. Cover loosely with foil and allow the steaks to rest and the cheese to melt for about 5 minutes. Sprinkle over the pancetta and serve with the jam on the side.

MUSTARD-GLAZED PORK TENDERLOIN
WITH DATE-SAGE RELISH

Pork tenderloin, a lovely little roast, is ideal for the grill because it cooks in just a few minutes and is congenial to a whole range of flavors. Here we coat it with spicy mustard seeds before it goes over the coals, then brush it with a pungent-sweet mix of honey and mustard just before it comes off the grill (so the honey doesn't burn). To round out the flavor palette, we serve the meat with an earthy and sweet date-sage relish.

Serves 4

THE MEAT

2 pork tenderloins, 12–14oz (350–400g) each
Kosher salt
3 tablespoons brown mustard seeds
3 tablespoons freshly cracked black pepper
3 tablespoons olive oil
¼ cup wholegrain mustard
¼ cup honey

THE RELISH

1 tablespoon freshly cracked coriander seeds (or substitute 1½ teaspoons ground coriander)
¼ cup pitted, diced dates
Juice of ½ orange (about ¼ cup)
Juice of I lemon (about ¼ cup)
¼ cup roughly chopped fresh parsley
2 tablespoons roughly chopped fresh sage
1 tablespoon peeled and minced fresh ginger
1 tablespoon finely minced orange zest

Build a fire in your grill. When the coals are all ignited, the fire has died down, and the temperature is medium (*see p34*), you're ready to cook.

Toast the coriander seeds for the relish, if using, in a dry skillet on the grill, shaking them frequently to avoid burning, until they become fragrant and are just a shade darker (3–5 minutes).

Dry the tenderloins well with paper towels and sprinkle generously with salt. Combine the mustard seeds, black pepper, and oil in a small bowl and mix well. Rub this mixture all over the meat, pressing gently to make it adhere.

Whisk the mustard and honey together in another small bowl until well blended.

Put the tenderloins on the grill over the coals and cook, rolling them around every 3–4 minutes for even cooking, until they are done to your liking (12–15 minutes for medium). Brush the tenderloins all over with the honey mustard during the last 30 seconds of cooking. To check for doneness, poke the meat with your finger to check its firmness (*see p37*). If you're unsure, make a cut in the thickest part of one of the tenderloins; it should be slightly less done than you like it. Transfer the tenderloins to a cutting board and cover them loosely with foil to keep warm.

While the tenderloins are resting, combine all the relish ingredients in a small bowl and toss gently.

Carve the pork into ½in (1cm) thick slices, and arrange these on a serving platter. Drizzle with the honey mustard, and pass the relish on the side.

HARISSA-RUBBED GRILLED SKIRT STEAK WITH ORANGE-FENNEL RELISH

This dish is for true heat fanatics. Although lamb would be more typically Moroccan, we think the fiery complexity of harissa and the bright, cooling flavors of this relish work perfectly with rich, meaty skirt steak too. If you're in a hurry or are not particularly fussy, you can just chop the oranges into chunks rather than peeling off all the membrane.

Serves 4

THE MEAT

2½lb (1kg) trimmed skirt steak, cut into 4 pieces
Kosher salt and freshly cracked black pepper

THE RELISH

1 fennel bulb, trimmed, cored, and finely sliced
1 large orange
2 tablespoons red wine vinegar
2 tablespoons roughly chopped fresh mint
Kosher salt and freshly cracked black pepper to taste

THE HARISSA

¼ cup olive oil
¼ cup red pepper flakes (or crushed dried red chiles of your choice)
2 tablespoons freshly cracked coriander seeds, toasted (see opposite), or substitute 1 tablespoon ground coriander
2 tablespoons cumin seed
1 tablespoon fennel seed
1 tablespoon minced fresh garlic

Build a multilevel fire in your grill (*see p31*). When the coals are all ignited, the fire has died down, and the temperature is medium (*see p34*), you're ready to cook.

Make the relish: On the stove top, bring a pan of salted water to a boil. Add the fennel and cook for 2 minutes. Drain well, and allow it to cool. Peel the orange with a sharp knife, removing all the white pith. Working over a bowl to catch the juice, cut between the section membranes and remove each orange section whole, discarding the seeds. Put the orange segments in another bowl. Measure 2 tablespoons of the juice, and add it to the orange segments, along with the blanched fennel, vinegar, mint, and salt and pepper. Mix well and set aside.

Make the harissa: Mash the oil, pepper flakes or chiles, coriander, cumin, fennel seed, and garlic into a paste. Dry the steaks well with paper towels, season them generously with salt and pepper, then rub the paste on both sides.

When the fire is ready, put the steaks on the grill over the hottest coals and sear them well on one side (about 4 minutes). Turn the steaks and continue to cook until done to your liking (4–5 minutes more for medium-rare). To check for doneness, poke each steak with your finger to test its firmness (*see p37*). If you're unsure, make a cut in the thickest part of one steak; it should be slightly less done than you like. Transfer the steaks to a cutting board, cover loosely with foil, and allow them to rest for 5 minutes.

Thinly slice the steaks on the bias across the grain and serve, with the relish on the side.

ASIAN-FLAVORED GRILLED BABY BACK PORK RIBS

The first time I (Chris) ever had ribs was in a Chinese restaurant in the Virginia town where I grew up. Even now, when I think of ribs the first thing that pops up in my flavor memory is the taste of those pupu platter favorites. But this updated version has deeper, more powerful flavors; plus, with its grill-and-toss approach, it's easier to make. If you're serving these as finger food at a party—for which they are perfect—you should make twice as many as you think you need, because they're going to disappear fast.

Serves 6 as an appetizer

THE MEAT

2 slabs baby back ribs, about 2lb (900g) each
2 tablespoons vegetable oil
Kosher salt and freshly cracked white pepper (or substitute black) to taste

THE SAUCE

⅓ cup finely crushed roasted peanuts
¼ cup roughly chopped scallions, green and white parts
¼ cup hoisin sauce
¼ cup soy sauce
¼ cup rice wine vinegar
3 tablespoons Asian sesame oil
2 tablespoons sriracha (Southeast Asian hot chile-garlic sauce, available in Asian markets or large supermarkets)
2 tablespoons peeled and minced fresh ginger

Light a fire well over to one side of your grill, using enough coals to fill half a shoebox.

Rub the ribs with oil and sprinkle them generously with salt and pepper.

When the fire has died down and the coals are covered in white ash, place the ribs on the side of the grill away from the coals, being careful that none of the meat is directly over the coals. Put the lid on the grill with the vents open one-quarter of the way and cook for 20 minutes. Flip the ribs and cook them for an additional 20 minutes.

Meanwhile, combine the ingredients for the sauce in a very large bowl and mix well.

When the ribs are done, transfer them to a cutting board. Cut the racks apart, adding the ribs to the bowl of sauce as they are separated. Toss the ribs with the sauce until thoroughly coated, and serve immediately—with lots of paper napkins.

WATER-DWELLERS

TAKE A LOOK AT THE BEACHES OF THE TROPICAL WORLD AND YOU'LL UNDERSTAND THE LONG-STANDING (AND VERY DELICIOUS) RELATIONSHIP BETWEEN SEAFOOD AND LIVE-FIRE COOKING. AND SINCE WE LOVE BEACHES AND TROPICS, WE ARE HUGE FANS OF FISH AND OTHER SEA CREATURES ON THE GRILL. WITH THESE RECIPES, WE THINK YOU WILL BE, TOO.

GRILL-SEARED DOUBLE-THICK TUNA STEAKS WITH PICKLED GINGER, WASABI, AND SOY

Twenty-two years ago, on the day that I (Chris) opened the doors of my restaurant, the East Coast Grill, in Cambridge, Massachusetts, this dish was on the menu. All these years later, it is still the most popular single item we serve. The key to this dish lies in its simplicity; the sole determining factor of success or failure is getting #1, super-fresh, sushi-quality tuna. Make sure that you cut it really thick and cook it the way you like your steak. We think it tastes best rare but, as with all food, it's your choice. Pickled ginger and wasabi should be available at a good Asian foodstore or larger supermarket. Alternatively, you can order from several specialty Japanese food item retailers online.

Serves 4

THE INGREDIENTS

¼ cup sesame seeds
4 hyper-fresh tuna steaks, about 3in (7.5cm) thick,
  8–10oz (225–280g) each
3 tablespoons Asian sesame oil
2 tablespoons freshly cracked white pepper
2 tablespoons kosher salt
4 scallions, ends trimmed, cut into thin strips
¼ cup pickled ginger
3 tablespoons wasabi powder, mixed with water to the
  consistency of wet sand
⅓ cup soy sauce, preferably the aged, dark kind

Build a fire in your grill. When the coals are all ignited, the flames have died down, and the temperature is hot (*see p34*), you're ready to cook.

Lightly toast the sesame seeds in a dry skillet on the grill, shaking them frequently to prevent burning, until they are just a shade darker. (You can alternatively do this over medium heat on the stove top.) Set them aside.

Rub the tuna steaks all over with the sesame oil, sprinkle with the white pepper and salt, then put them on the grill directly over the coals and sear well on both sides (4–5 minutes per side). When you have a dark brown, crispy crust on both sides, grill the steaks on each of the 4 edges for about 2 minutes, aiming to achieve the same dark, crusty effect. Transfer to a serving platter or individual plates.

Scatter the scallions and sesame seeds over the tuna, and serve with the pickled ginger, wasabi, and soy sauce on the side.

SIMPLE BRICK-GRILLED SQUID
WITH LEMON, CHILE, AND GARLIC

Here we take a technique that is typically used with chicken—holding it flat against the grill with a brick, so that it gets a really nice overall sear from the flames—and apply it to squid. This has the added advantage of making sure that the squid cooks really quickly, which keeps it from toughening up. Plus, it's always fun to have guests wondering why you need a foil-wrapped brick to make dinner.

Serves 4 as an appetizer

THE SQUID

1½lb (675g) cleaned squid with tentacles (separate these from the squid bodies, or ask your fishmonger to do so), thoroughly rinsed and drained well

2 tablespoons olive oil

1 tablespoon red pepper flakes

Kosher salt and freshly cracked black pepper to taste

THE DRESSING

⅓ cup roughly chopped fresh cilantro

¼ cup extra virgin olive oil

Juice of 1 lemon (about ¼ cup)

1 teaspoon minced garlic

7 dashes Tabasco sauce, or to taste

Build a fire in your grill. When the coals are all ignited, the fire has died down, and the temperature is hot (*see p34*), you're ready to cook. Wrap a clean brick with foil and place it by your grill.

Put the squid in a large bowl, add the olive oil, red pepper flakes, and salt and pepper, and toss gently to coat. Thread the tentacles onto skewers so they don't fall through the grill when you cook them.

Combine the cilantro, olive oil, lemon juice, garlic, and Tabasco in a large bowl. Mix well and set aside.

Arrange a few squid bodies on the grill over the coals, and cover them completely with the brick. Cook until opaque throughout, about 2 minutes per side, then remove the brick and allow the bodies to cook for about 30 seconds longer, until they are golden brown and crispy. Repeat this process with the rest of the squid bodies, adding the tentacles to the grill (no brick required) with the last batch. Cook the tentacles for about 2 minutes, until they are evenly brown and crispy.

Slice the squid bodies into rings and add them, along with the tentacles, to the lemon-garlic dressing, tossing to coat. Pile the squid onto a platter and serve.

PORTUGAL: THE FISH THAT CHANGED IT ALL

When people ask, as they sometimes do, what is the best meal I (Doc) have ever eaten, one of the top contenders is a very simple lunch I had years ago on the beach in southern Portugal.

I was traveling with friends and, since we were on a very strict budget, we decided to camp out on the beach instead of staying in a hotel. Fortunately, not far from our makeshift campsite was a small, open-air restaurant, really nothing more than a handful of tables with a roof over them, right on the sand. There wasn't much in the way of equipment—a wood-burning grill, a hot plate, and a large cooler—and when we arrived there didn't seem to be much food, either. It looked like some greens and maybe some fried potatoes were about all we could look forward to. But there was cold white wine in the cooler, and it was a beautiful day, so we settled in. Unfortunately, we couldn't seem to get our hosts to serve us any food. After about half an hour, though, we discovered why: The entrée was just arriving. A small fishing boat pulled up right on the beach and several men jumped out and brought pails of fish up the dunes. The young cook paid for them, quickly cleaned them, and threw them on the wood fire that he had built up when the boat came into sight. I must admit, though, that I was a little apprehensive. These fish, I was told by my friends, were sardines, and I had never been a fan of dark-fleshed, oily fish. But this meal changed that forever. The salad was crisp and refreshing, the potatoes earthy and satisfying, but the sardines stole the show. Hot off the grill, with crispy skin and rich, dark, succulent flesh, they were a revelation. Oily fish became my friends, and still are to this day.

SIMPLE GRILLED SARDINES
WITH LEMON AND PAPRIKA

Fresh sardines are wonderful fish for the grill, with a delicious, meaty taste. Here we simply top them with some traditional Portuguese flavors, then grill them up. For a slightly more exotic approach, try replacing the regular paprika with *pimentón de La Vera*, a Spanish smoked paprika with a distinctive smoky flavor.

Serves 4 as an appetizer

¼ cup extra virgin olive oil
1 teaspoon minced garlic
1 teaspoon good-quality paprika
12 fresh sardines
2 lemons, one halved and one cut into quarters
¼ cup roughly chopped fresh parsley
Kosher salt and freshly cracked black pepper

Build a fire in your grill. When the coals are all ignited, the flames have died down, and the temperature is hot (*see p34*), you're ready to cook.

Mix together the olive oil, garlic, and paprika in a small bowl. Pour this mixture over the sardines, then squeeze the two lemon halves over them and sprinkle with the parsley and salt and pepper to taste.

Put the sardines on the grill directly over the coals and cook until they are nicely seared on the outside and just opaque on the inside (3–4 minutes per side). To check for doneness, manipulate one of the sardines so you can see inside it at its thickest point to be sure it is just opaque all the way through.

Serve with lemon quarters for squeezing.

GRILLED CUMIN-CRUSTED SALMON FILLETS WITH ORANGE-CHIPOTLE BUTTER

Salmon works perfectly on the grill, because it has a firm enough texture not to fall apart, and its strong, rich, defined taste can stand up to the grill flavor. Here we challenge the salmon further with a quick cumin rub and a flavored butter featuring the hot, smoky chipotle pepper along with a combination of other Latin ingredients. Fortunately, the fish is up to the challenge, and the resulting dish is spectacular.

Serves 4

THE FISH

3 tablespoons freshly cracked cumin seeds (or substitute 1½ tablespoons ground cumin)

4 salmon fillets, about 8oz (225g) each (or substitute mahi-mahi, bluefish, or halibut)

2 tablespoons olive oil

Kosher salt and freshly cracked black pepper to taste

THE BUTTER

2 tablespoons minced canned or jarred chipotle peppers in adobo sauce

2 tablespoons roughly chopped fresh cilantro

Juice of 1 lime (about 2 tablespoons)

1 tablespoon finely minced orange zest

4 tablespoons unsalted butter, softened

Kosher salt and freshly cracked black pepper

Make the butter: Combine the chipotles, cilantro, lime juice, orange zest, and butter in a small bowl and mash together until evenly blended. Add salt and pepper to taste. Wrap the butter in plastic wrap, shape it into a log, and refrigerate until firm. (This butter will keep in the refrigerator for a week, or frozen for several months.)

Toast the cumin seeds (if using) on the stove top in a dry skillet over medium heat, shaking them frequently to prevent burning, until they are fragrant and just a shade darker (3–5 minutes). Set them aside.

Build a fire in your grill. When the coals are all ignited, the flames have died down, and the temperature is medium (see p34), you're ready to cook.

Rub the salmon fillets on both sides with olive oil, sprinkle generously with salt and pepper, then rub the cumin into the salmon, pressing gently so it adheres. Put the fillets on the grill over the coals and cook until almost opaque throughout (6–8 minutes per side). To check for doneness, poke the fish with your finger to test its firmness (see p37). If you're unsure, make a cut in the thickest part of the fillet to be sure it is nearly opaque all the way through. Transfer the salmon to a platter, and top each hot fillet with a slice or two of the seasoned butter.

PEPPER-CRUSTED GRILLED SWORDFISH
WITH SMOKED SALMON-CHIVE BUTTER

If you're apprehensive about grilling fish, this recipe is a great one for sharpening your skills. The solid, meaty texture of swordfish makes it ideal for the grill—it's really no more difficult than a steak—and its mild-tasting white flesh is ideal for pairing with a range of distinct flavors. Plus, if you make the salmon-chive butter in advance (it keeps in the refrigerator for several days, and in the freezer for a couple of months), you can come home from work and have this dish on the table in no time at all.

Serves 4

THE FISH

4 swordfish steaks, about 1in (2.5cm) thick, 8oz (225g) each

2 tablespoons olive oil

3 tablespoons freshly cracked black pepper

1 tablespoon kosher salt

THE BUTTER

½ cup unsalted butter, softened

2oz (60g) smoked salmon, roughly chopped

Juice of ½ a lemon (about 2 tablespoons)

5 dashes Tabasco sauce

3 tablespoons minced fresh chives

Kosher salt and freshly cracked black pepper to taste

Build a fire in your grill. When the coals are all ignited, the flames have died down, and the temperature is hot (*see p34*), you're ready to cook.

Rub the fish steaks with the oil and coat them generously with the pepper and salt, pressing gently so it adheres. Put the steaks on the grill directly over the coals and cook until they are just opaque throughout (5–7 minutes per side). To check for doneness, poke the fish with your finger to test its firmness (*see p37*); if you're unsure, make a cut in one of the steaks to be sure it is just opaque all the way through.

While the swordfish is on the grill, combine the butter, salmon, lemon juice, and Tabasco in a food processor and blend until smooth. Add the chives and salt and pepper to taste and pulse a few times to blend.

When the fish is done, arrange the steaks on a platter, top each one with some of the salmon-chive butter, and serve immediately.

GRILLED STRIPED BASS
WITH MEDITERRANEAN SALAD

We are lucky enough to spend a lot of time on the southern coast of Massachusetts, and (when we're even luckier) we sometimes catch striped bass there. This simple summer dish is one of our favorite ways to prepare it—the subtly-flavored, big-flaked fish is perfect grilled very plainly (*see overleaf*), then nicely complemented by the restrained flavors of the tomato-cucumber salad. If you can't get ahold of striped bass, sea bass is just as delicious prepared this way.

Serves 4

THE FISH

4 striped bass fillets, 8oz (225g) each
2 tablespoons vegetable oil
Kosher salt and freshly cracked black pepper

THE SALAD

2 tomatoes about the size of baseballs, cored and diced large
1 cucumber, peeled if desired, diced medium
½ red onion, peeled and diced small
⅓ cup pitted black olives

THE DRESSING

Juice of 1½ lemons (about ⅓ cup)
¼ cup minced fresh basil
Pinch of red pepper flakes
Kosher salt and freshly cracked black pepper to taste
⅓ cup extra virgin olive oil

Build a multilevel fire (*see p31*) in your grill. When the coals are all ignited, the flames have died down, and the temperature is medium (*see p34*), you're ready to cook.

Rub the bass fillets with the vegetable oil and sprinkle them generously with salt and pepper. Place the fillets on the hotter side of the grill and cook until they develop a crusty, dark sear on the outside and are opaque on the inside (6–8 minutes per side). If the flesh starts to become too dark, move the fillets to the cooler side of the grill and cover them with a pie plate or disposable foil pan to finish cooking. To check for doneness, poke the fish with your finger to test its firmness (*see p37*); if you're unsure, make a cut in one of the fillets to be sure it is just opaque all the way through.

While the fish is cooking, put the salad ingredients in a medium-sized bowl. Combine all the dressing ingredients except the olive oil in a small bowl, then add the oil, whisking, and whisk until well blended. Add just enough of this dressing to moisten the salad mixture and toss until well blended and evenly coated with dressing.

To serve, divide the salad among four dinner plates and arrange a grilled fillet over each.

GRILLED OYSTERS ON THE HALF-SHELL
WITH PANCETTA AND BARBECUE SAUCE

Some people eat only raw oysters; others eat only cooked ones. We happen to be members of both clubs. This dish is in the great grilled oyster tradition that's found in the bays and inlets of the Pacific coast north of San Francisco, where you can go buy a bag of oysters and a bag of charcoal and cook 'em yourself right on the scene. There's not much that's better than that. Here we accompany the oysters with a simple barbecue sauce and, in keeping with our belief that almost anything goes better with a little cured pork, top them with some pancetta.

Serves 4 as an appetizer

THE INGREDIENTS

8oz (225g) pancetta, diced small
3 tablespoons butter
¼ cup ketchup
Juice of 1 lemon (about ¼ cup)
2 tablespoons roughly chopped fresh parsley
6 dashes Tabasco sauce
3 dashes Worcestershire sauce
Kosher salt and freshly cracked black pepper to taste
24 oysters of your choice, shells scrubbed

Build a fire in your grill. When the coals are all ignited, the fire has died down, and the temperature is medium (*see p34*), you're ready to cook.

While you wait for the fire, cook the pancetta on the stove top in a large sauté pan over medium-low heat, stirring frequently until it is crisp and brown (about 7 minutes). Transfer to paper towels to drain.

Melt the butter in a small saucepan. Whisk in the ketchup, lemon juice, half of the parsley (reserve the rest for garnishing), Tabasco, Worcestershire sauce, and salt and pepper, and remove from the heat.

Shuck the oysters and loosen them in their bottom shells. Arrange the oysters (in their bottom shells) on the grill over the coals, and cook just until their edges start to ruffle (2–3 minutes). Spoon about 1 tablespoon sauce over each oyster, and continue to cook until the sauce is bubbling hot. Transfer to a serving platter, sprinkle with parsley and pancetta, and serve, but be careful—the oyster shells will be very hot.

GRILLED "CAJUN-STYLE" GROUPER
WITH TABASCO-CORN TARTAR SAUCE

Back in the 1980s, Cajun cooking suddenly became very popular in the US, and everyone wanted blackened redfish. This is our version of that approach, in which fish is coated with a spice rub and put over the fire to blacken the mixture, which gives the fish a nice crust. (If you can't find grouper, you can substitute catfish, tilefish, flounder, or snapper.) And the spicy tartar sauce, with the nice crunch of corn kernels and the sweetness of pickle relish, goes with just about any white-fleshed fish, however it's prepared.

Serves 4

THE FISH

3 tablespoons paprika

2 tablespoons ground coriander

2 tablespoons kosher salt

1 tablespoon dry mustard

1 tablespoon ground black pepper

1 tablespoon cayenne pepper

4 grouper steaks or fillets, 8–10oz (225–280g) each

3 tablespoons olive oil

THE SAUCE

1 ear corn, husked and desilked

⅔ cup mayonnaise

¼ cup storebought sweet pickle relish

3 tablespoons roughly chopped fresh parsley

2–3 tablespoons Tabasco (or other hot sauce of your choice), or use as much or little as you prefer

2 tablespoons prepared brown mustard

1 tablespoon celery seeds

Kosher salt and freshly cracked black pepper to taste

For the sauce: On the stove top, bring a large pan of salted water to a boil and blanch the ear of corn for 2 minutes. Drain and cut the kernels off the cob (it should yield about ¼ cup).

Combine the corn kernels with the rest of the sauce ingredients in a small bowl and mix well. Transfer to a serving bowl, cover, and refrigerate until serving time.

Build a fire in your grill. When the coals are all ignited, the flames have died down, and the temperature is medium (*see p34*), you're ready to cook.

Combine the paprika, coriander, kosher salt, dry mustard, black pepper, and cayenne pepper in a small bowl and mix well. Rub the grouper with olive oil and coat it generously on all sides with the spice mixture, pressing gently to be sure it adheres. Put the fish on the grill directly over the coals and cook until it is just opaque throughout (6–8 minutes per side). To check for doneness, poke the fish with your finger to test its firmness (*see p37*); if you're unsure, make a cut in one of the steaks or fillets to be sure it is opaque all the way through.

Transfer the fish to a platter and serve, passing the tartar sauce on the side.

GRILLED MONKFISH WITH LATIN FLAVORS

The dense, meaty texture and mild, sweetish flavor of monkfish have made it a favorite of grillers. Although it is often called "poor man's lobster," it is actually more able to stand up to strong flavors than lobster is. In this simple dish we take advantage of that trait by coating the fish with cumin and coriander before it goes over the coals, then drizzling it with a spicy vinaigrette that features flavors of Latin America.

Serves 4

THE FISH

3 tablespoons freshly cracked cumin seeds
2 tablespoons ground coriander
Kosher salt and freshly cracked black pepper to taste
4 monkfish fillets, about 8oz (225g) each
2 tablespoons olive oil

THE VINAIGRETTE

⅓ cup extra virgin olive oil
Juice of 2 limes (about ¼ cup)
3 tablespoons roughly chopped fresh oregano
1 tablespoon minced fresh chile pepper of your choice, or to taste
1 teaspoon minced fresh garlic
Kosher salt and freshly cracked black pepper to taste

Build a fire in your grill. When the coals are all ignited, the flames have died down, and the temperature is medium-hot (*see p34*), you're ready to cook.

Combine the cumin, coriander, and salt and pepper in a small bowl and mix well. Rub the fillets with the oil and coat them generously with this mixture, pressing gently so it adheres. Put on the grill and cook until just opaque throughout (6–8 minutes per side). To check for doneness, poke the fish with your finger to test its firmness (*see p37*); if you're unsure, make a cut in one of the fillets to be sure it is just opaque all the way through.

While the fish is on the grill, combine the vinaigrette ingredients in a small bowl and whisk until well blended.

Transfer the fillets to a serving platter, drizzle generously with vinaigrette, and serve, passing the remaining vinaigrette on the side.

FLAVOR FOOTPRINT SOUTHEAST ASIA

Over the past couple of decades, the cuisines of Southeast Asia have truly come into their own on the international culinary stage. Perhaps their most salient characteristic is a tendency to combine hot, sour, sweet, and salty all in the same dish, so that each mouthful is a kaleidoscope of flavors. Often this riot of tastes is deepened and united by the judicious use of fermented seafood products, of which fish sauce (stocked by most large supermarkets) is perhaps the most amenable to Western taste buds; if you want to experiment with others, check out your local Southeast Asian grocery. We love the explosive nature of Southeast Asian flavors, and after you try out a couple of these easy condiments, we think you will, too.

Southeast Asian-Style Spice Paste
Makes about 1 cup

Brush or rub this fiery curry paste all over any cut of lamb or beef before grilling.

2 tablespoons Asian sesame oil
3 tablespoons vegetable oil
2 tablespoons crushed coriander seeds
¼ cup minced jalapeño or other fresh chile pepper
   of your choice
2 tablespoons peeled and minced fresh ginger
2 stalks lemongrass, finely minced (use the tender
   inner portion of the bottom third of the stalk only)
2 tablespoons minced fresh garlic
1 tablespoon ground white pepper
2 teaspoons kosher salt

Combine all the ingredients in a small bowl and mix well or, if you prefer a finer paste, crush together in a mortar and pestle, still leaving it somewhat chunky. This paste will keep, covered and refrigerated, for 2–3 days.

Southeast Asian Spice Rub
Makes about 1 cup

Rub this dry spice mixture on any large piece of meat or fowl that you're going to grill.

¼ cup curry powder
¼ cup ground coriander
2 tablespoons ground cumin
2 tablespoons ground white pepper
2 tablespoons kosher salt
1 tablespoon turmeric
1 tablespoon ground ginger
1 tablespoon cayenne pepper

Combine all the ingredients in a small bowl and mix well. Stored in an airtight container in a cool, dark place, this rub will keep for months.

Southeast Asian-
Style Spice Paste

Chile-Fish Sauce Condiment
Makes about 1 cup

A simple but versatile dipping sauce to accompany skewers of chicken, fish, shrimp, or pork.

⅓ cup Southeast Asian fish sauce
Juice of 3 limes (about 6 tablespoons)
2 jalapeños or other fresh chile pepper of your choice, sliced into thin circles
2 teaspoons granulated sugar

Combine all the ingredients in a small bowl and mix until the sugar dissolves. This condiment will keep, covered and refrigerated, for 4–5 days.

Mango-Ginger Relish
Makes about 2 cups

This relish is a great accompaniment to just about anything grilled, but we particularly like it with seafood or chicken.

1 large, ripe but firm mango, peeled, pitted, and diced small (should yield about 1½ cups)
¼ cup roughly chopped scallions, including green tops
Juice of 2 limes (about ¼ cup)
2 tablespoons peeled and minced fresh ginger
2 tablespoons Southeast Asian fish sauce
1 tablespoon minced fresh chile pepper of your choice

Combine all the ingredients in a medium bowl and mix well. This relish will keep, covered and refrigerated, for 2–3 days.

Peach-Chile Sambal
Makes about 1¼ cups

The chile-fired condiments called sambals originated in Malaysia and Indonesia, but are now found all over Southeast Asia as well as southern Africa. This peach-based version is great with pork, lamb, or full-flavored fish like mackerel or bluefish.

2 ripe but firm peaches, peeled, pitted, and diced small
2 tablespoons minced fresh jalapeño or other fresh chile pepper of your choice
2 tablespoons roughly chopped fresh cilantro
2 tablespoons fish sauce
1 tablespoon peeled and minced fresh ginger
Juice of 1½ limes (about 3 tablespoons)
1 teaspoon granulated sugar

Combine all the ingredients in a medium bowl and mix well. Serve this one right away; the peaches won't hold up too long.

Mango-Ginger Relish

SIGNATURE INGREDIENTS/TOP ROW (LEFT TO RIGHT) Cilantro, coriander seeds, fish sauce, lemongrass; **SECOND ROW** Lime leaves, garlic, red shallots, Thai basil; **THIRD ROW** Mint, dried shrimp, ginger, tamarind; **BOTTOM ROW** Chiles, coconut milk, shrimp paste, galangal.

GRILLED HALIBUT
WITH LIME-CHIPOTLE MAYO AND SPICY PECANS

Mayonnaise and fish might seem like an odd combo, but once you taste this version, we think you'll understand why it's a classic. If you like, you can prepare both the mayonnaise mixture and the pecans in advance. Keep the mayo refrigerated and the pecans at room temperature, then all you'll have to do when your guests arrive is grill the halibut and you're ready to go. (The spicy pecans make a great snack on their own, by the way.)

Serves 4

THE FISH

4 halibut steaks, about 8oz (225g) each
2 tablespoons olive oil
Kosher salt and freshly cracked black pepper

THE MAYO

1 cup prepared mayonnaise
Juice of 1 lime (about 2 tablespoons)
2 tablespoons roughly chopped fresh cilantro
1 chipotle pepper in adobo sauce, minced

THE PECANS

⅓ cup pecans, lightly crushed
1 teaspoon olive oil
Pinch granulated sugar
Pinch chile powder
Pinch ground cumin
Pinch cayenne pepper
Kosher salt and freshly cracked black pepper to taste

Build a fire in your grill. When the coals are all ignited, the flames have died down, and the temperature is medium-hot (*see p34*), you're ready to cook.

In the meantime, combine the mayonnaise, lime juice, cilantro, and chipotle in a small bowl and mix well.

Combine the pecans, oil, sugar, and spices in a small sauté pan or skillet and toast on the stove top over medium heat, stirring frequently, just until fragrant (about 5 minutes). Transfer to a small bowl to cool.

Rub the halibut with oil and sprinkle it generously with salt and pepper, then put it on the grill directly over the coals and cook until it is just opaque throughout (5–6 minutes per side). To check for doneness, poke the fish with your finger to test its firmness (*see p37*); if you're unsure, make a cut in one of the steaks at its thickest point to be sure it is just opaque all the way through.

Arrange the halibut steaks on a platter, drizzle generously with the mayo, and scatter the pecans over the top.

GRILLED MAHI-MAHI
WITH AVOCADO-CORN SALSA

This subtropical fish ranges so widely in the ocean that is has several names—we call it by its Hawaiian name, which means "strong-strong," but it's also known as "dorado" and as "dolphinfish" because it often swims with dolphins. It is perhaps the most beautiful of game fish; when just out of the water, it displays a range of electric blues and greens and bright golds and silvers. It's also wonderful on the grill—mild-tasting, with a large, tender flake.

Serves 4 as an appetizer

THE FISH

1 tablespoon each: chile powder, ground cumin, and ground coriander

4 mahi-mahi fillets, about 8oz (225g) each (or substitute salmon, halibut, or cod fillet)

2 tablespoons olive oil

Kosher salt and freshly cracked black pepper

THE SALSA

2 ears corn, shucked

1 ripe but firm California avocado, pitted, peeled, and diced small

Juice of 3 limes (about ⅓ cup)

¼ cup roughly chopped fresh cilantro

3 tablespoons olive oil

1 teaspoon minced jalapeño or other fresh chile pepper of your choice

Kosher salt and freshly cracked black pepper to taste

Blanch the corn for the salsa: On the stove top, bring a large pan of salted water to the boil. Cook the ears for 2 minutes, drain, and cut the kernels off the cobs (should yield about 1 cup of kernels).

Combine the salsa ingredients in a medium bowl and mix gently but thoroughly. Cover with plastic wrap and refrigerate until serving time.

Build a fire in your grill. When the coals are all ignited, the flames have died down, and the temperature is medium-hot (*see p34*), you're ready to cook.

Combine the chile powder, cumin, and coriander in a small bowl and mix well. Rub the fish fillets on both sides with oil, sprinkle generously with salt and pepper, and rub all over with the spice mixture. Put the fillets over the coals and cook until just opaque all the way through (5–6 minutes per side). To check for doneness, poke the fish with your finger to test its firmness level (*see p37*); if you're unsure, make a cut in one of the fillets at its thickest point to be sure it is just opaque all the way through.

When the fish is done, put a fish fillet on each plate, top with a spoonful of the salsa, and pass the remaining salsa on the side.

GRILLED PEEL 'N' EAT SHRIMP
WITH OLD BAY, BASIL, AND LEMON

Here's a celebration of the intimacy and informality of eating with your fingers. I (Chris) grew up in the mid-Atlantic, and as a youth attended many a shrimp boil, where the flavoring trick was to dump the distinctive spice mixture called Old Bay Seasoning into the water that the seafood was cooked in. Here we ring a little change on that tradition by grilling the shrimp first, then tossing them with a flavorful mixture featuring Old Bay. Try this one with a super-cold beer.

Serves 4 as an appetizer

THE INGREDIENTS

1lb (450g) medium-large (16/20 per pound) shrimp,
   rinsed and drained
2 tablespoons olive oil
Kosher salt and freshly cracked black pepper to taste
Juice of 2 lemons (about ½ cup)
¼ cup roughly chopped fresh basil
3 tablespoons butter, at room temperature
2 tablespoons minced garlic
1 tablespoon Old Bay Seasoning
6 dashes Tabasco sauce
Kosher salt and freshly cracked black pepper to taste

Build a fire in your grill. When the coals are all ignited, the fire has died down, and the temperature is medium (*see p34*), you're ready to cook.

Using a small, sharp knife or small scissors, slit the shell along the back of each shrimp, and remove the vein.

Toss the shrimp with the oil and salt and pepper in a large bowl. Put the shrimp on the grill over the coals and cook until they are opaque throughout (4–5 minutes per side). To check for doneness, cut into one of the shrimp at its thickest point to be sure it is opaque all the way through.

While the shrimp are cooking, combine the lemon juice, basil, butter, garlic, Old Bay Seasoning, Tabasco, and salt and pepper in a large bowl and mix together well. When the shrimp are done, add them to the bowl and toss gently until the butter is melted and the shrimp are nicely coated. Serve the shrimp right out of the bowl, with another big bowl on the side for the shells.

CORIANDER-CRUSTED GRILLED HALIBUT STEAKS WITH FRESH TOMATO-MINT CHUTNEY

A firm-textured white fish with a large flake, halibut has a delicate flavor that calls for a relatively light preparation, so here we pair it with a range of light, bright, citrusy flavors. This is a very adaptable approach, which means that if you can't find halibut, you can substitute other white-fleshed fish such as haddock, hake, or cod in this recipe.

Serves 4

THE FISH

¼ cup freshly cracked coriander seeds
2 teaspoons freshly cracked white pepper
1 tablespoon kosher salt
4 halibut steaks about 1in (2.5cm) thick, 8–10oz (225–280g) each
2 tablespoons olive oil

THE CHUTNEY

2 ripe tomatoes, each about the size of a baseball, cored and diced medium (about 1½ cups)
¼ of a medium cucumber, diced medium (about ½ cup)
Juice of 2 lemons (about ½ cup)
¼ cup roughly chopped fresh mint
2 tablespoons peeled and minced fresh ginger
1 tablespoon Asian sesame oil
1 tablespoon minced fresh chile pepper of your choice
Kosher salt and freshly cracked black pepper to taste

Build a fire in your grill. When the coals are all ignited, the flames have died down, and the temperature is medium-hot (*see p34*), you're ready to cook.

Combine the coriander, white pepper, and salt in a small bowl and mix well. Rub the halibut with the oil and coat with the coriander mixture, pressing gently so it adheres. Put the fish on the grill directly over the coals and cook until it is just opaque throughout (5–6 minutes per side). To check for doneness, poke the fish with your finger to test its firmness (*see p37*); if you're unsure, make a cut in one of the steaks to be sure it is just opaque all the way through.

While the fish is on the grill, combine the chutney ingredients in a small bowl and toss until well mixed.

Arrange the halibut steaks on a platter, top each one with a spoonful of the chutney, and serve, passing the remaining chutney on the side.

GRILLED SCALLOP COCKTAIL

This is a take on ceviche, the classic Latin American dish in which fish is "cooked" by marinating it in citrus juice. Here we lightly grill the scallops before putting them in the lime environment, which they take to like—well, like a fish to water. To make a more substantial appetizer, we add tomato, avocado, and hearts of palm. This would also make a very delicious and cooling summer lunch for you and a friend.

Serves 4 as an appetizer

THE SALAD

3 tablespoons cumin seeds
1 baseball-sized tomato, cored and diced small
1 ripe but firm avocado, pitted, peeled, and diced small, and lightly coated with fresh lemon juice
½ cup ¼ in (5mm) thick slices hearts of palm
½ head romaine lettuce, cut crosswise into thin strips

THE DRESSING

Juice of 3 limes (about ⅓ cup)
¼ cup extra virgin olive oil
2 tablespoons minced fresh chile pepper of your choice
2 tablespoons roughly chopped fresh oregano
1 teaspoon minced fresh garlic
Kosher salt and freshly cracked black pepper to taste

THE SCALLOPS

1lb (450g) large sea scallops (about 16), cleaned
2 tablespoons vegetable oil
1 tablespoon ground cumin
Kosher salt and freshly cracked black pepper to taste

On the stove top, toast the cumin seeds in a dry skillet over medium heat, shaking frequently to avoid burning, until fragrant and just a shade darker (2–3 minutes). Crack them in a pestle and mortar or with the base of a heavy pan.

Build a fire in your grill. When the coals are all ignited, the flames have died down, and the temperature is medium (*see p34*), you're ready to cook.

Put the tomato, avocado, and hearts of palm in a large bowl; set aside. Combine the lime juice, olive oil, chiles, oregano, garlic, and salt and pepper in a small bowl, and whisk until well blended. Set aside.

Rub the scallops with the vegetable oil and sprinkle them with the cumin and salt and pepper to taste. Put them on the grill directly over the coals and cook until they are just opaque throughout (3–4 minutes per side). To check for doneness, make a cut in one of the largest scallops to be sure it is opaque all the way through.

Transfer the cooked scallops to the bowl with the tomato mixture. Whisk the dressing again to blend, add just enough to moisten the scallops and vegetables, and toss until evenly coated.

To serve, divide the lettuce among four salad plates, spoon a quarter of the scallop mixture on top of each, and sprinkle with the toasted cumin seeds.

MOROCCO: THE CHARMS OF THE COAST

If you had to pick the most well-known image of Morocco, it would be of the Djemaa el Fna, the kaleidoscopic central square of Marrakech. At night, especially, it is ablaze with excitement: the calls of snake charmers and water sellers, the sparkling robes of magicians, the jostling of huge crowds, and everywhere the smoke of grilling fires. But Morocco has a more tranquil side.

In little-known Rabat, the country's capital and administrative hub, things are very different. In fact, this rather sedate city is not a place we would have stopped at by design. But a number of years ago we ended up spending several days there waiting to get visas to enter Algeria (rather difficult to come by at the time, since the two countries were engaged in a border skirmish). Over the course of our visit, we slowly became enamored of the gentle graces of the city—the spacious boulevards and gardens, the art deco mansions in the colonial quarter, the grand Mausoleum of Mohammed V, the small but suitably exotic medina. This was a city for strolling, free of the frenetic traffic and relentless touts that can make Marrakech and Fez difficult to negotiate. Best of all, though, were the seaside restaurants. Our particular favorite was a modest place, about a dozen tables set in single file along the sea, with brilliant fuchsia bougainvillea climbing the cracked walls. It was there that we first discovered *charmoula*. Draped across a procession of super-fresh fish that had spent just the proper amount of time on a charcoal-fired grill, this classic, slightly aggressive herb sauce was the ideal complement to the sweetish, lightly smoky seafood. We returned each afternoon to sit in the sun, listen to the waves, and learn from the masters how fish and strong tastes can perform perfectly together.

MOROCCAN-STYLE GRILLED SEA SCALLOPS WITH SPICY GREEN SAUCE

The green herb sauce in this dish is our spin on Moroccan *charmoula*, which is typically served with seafood. We love it not just because it's delicious, but also because it's a perfect example of how strong, aggressive flavors can match up very well with seafood, promoting the subtle flavor of the fish rather than overpowering it. To expand the concept, we enliven the large sea scallops we use here with a cumin-coriander crust.

Serves 4

2lb (900g) large sea scallops (about 24 scallops)
¼ cup olive oil
2 tablespoons cumin seeds
1 tablespoon ground coriander
1 tablespoon paprika
Kosher salt and freshly cracked black pepper to taste

For the sauce:
¾ cup roughly chopped fresh cilantro
¼ cup roughly chopped fresh parsley
¼ cup extra virgin olive oil
2 tablespoons red wine vinegar
3 garlic cloves, peeled
1 teaspoon red pepper flakes

Build a fire in your grill. When the coals are all ignited, the fire has died down, and the temperature is hot (*see p34*), you're ready to cook.

Combine all of the sauce ingredients in a food processor or blender and purée until smooth. Transfer to a serving bowl and set aside.

Combine the scallops, olive oil, cumin, coriander, paprika, and salt and pepper in a large bowl; toss gently until the scallops are evenly coated with the other ingredients. Put the scallops on the grill over the coals and cook until just opaque throughout (3–4 minutes per side). To check for doneness, cut into one of the scallops to be sure it is just opaque all the way through.

To serve, divide the scallops among 4 plates and drizzle with the sauce. Pass the remaining sauce on the side.

GRILLED MONKFISH WITH CRABMEAT, CRISPY PROSCIUTTO, AND ARTICHOKE HEARTS

Mild-flavored grilled monkfish provides the perfect foil for a trio of Italian ingredients with deep, rich flavors—mellow crabmeat, crisp, salty ham, and delicately nutty artichoke hearts. If you have the time and the inclination, fresh artichoke hearts are particularly tasty (see Grilled Artichoke, Arugula, and Radicchio Salad on p258 for how to prepare them), but jarred ones work well here, too.

Serves 4

THE INGREDIENTS

4 monkfish fillets, about 8oz (225g) each
2 tablespoons vegetable oil
Kosher salt and freshly cracked black pepper
12 thin slices prosciutto
4 jarred or cooked fresh artichoke hearts, quartered
8oz (225g) fresh lump crabmeat, carefully picked over
Juice of 1 lemon (about ¼ cup)
¼ cup roughly chopped fresh parsley
3 tablespoons extra virgin olive oil

Build a fire in your grill. When the coals are all ignited, the flames have died down, and the temperature is medium-hot (see p34), you're ready to cook.

Rub the monkfish with the vegetable oil and sprinkle it generously with salt and pepper. Put it on the grill directly over the coals and cook until just opaque throughout (6–8 minutes per side). To check for doneness, poke the fish with your finger to test its firmness (see p37); if you're unsure, make a cut in one of the fillets to be sure it is just opaque all the way through.

Meanwhile, put the prosciutto on the grill around the edge of the fire and cook until it starts to brown and crisp at the edges (about 1 minute per side).

Put the artichoke hearts and crabmeat in a medium bowl and sprinkle with the lemon juice, parsley, and extra virgin olive oil. Add salt and pepper to taste, and toss gently to blend.

Arrange the fish fillets on a serving platter, spoon the crab mixture on top, break up the prosciutto over the crab, and serve immediately.

CUMIN-CRUSTED GRILLED SALMON
WITH CUCUMBER-GREEN CHILE SALSA

Earthy cumin makes a really nice combination with salmon, which has enough flavor of its own to stand up to the spice. Using seeds rather than powdered cumin also gives you a crunchy crust that's a lovely contrast with the tender fish. This recipe was perfected by East Coast Grill chef Jason Lord at his famed Latin Sunday brunch. The summery salsa is also delicious with any other flavorful fish, such as bluefish, tuna, or even sardines.

Serves 4

THE FISH

4 skin-on salmon fillets, about 8oz (225g) each
2 tablespoons olive oil
2 tablespoons cumin seeds, freshly cracked
Kosher salt and freshly cracked black pepper to taste

THE SALSA

½ cucumber, diced small (about 1 cup)
½ cup small-diced Fresno or other mild green chile peppers (or use less or more to taste)
¼ cup roughly chopped fresh cilantro
Juice of 2 limes (about ¼ cup)
1 teaspoon ground cumin
1 teaspoon ground coriander
1 teaspoon chile powder
Kosher salt and freshly cracked black pepper to taste

Build a fire in your grill. When the coals are all ignited, the fire has died down, and the temperature is medium (*see p34*), you're ready to cook.

Rub the salmon fillets on both sides with oil and coat them generously with cumin and salt and pepper, pressing gently to be sure the seasonings adhere. Put the fillets on the grill skin side down and cook, turning once, until they are just opaque throughout (6–8 minutes per side). To check for doneness, poke the fish with your finger to test its firmness (*see p37*); if you're unsure, cut into one of the fillets at its thickest point to be sure it is opaque all the way through.

While the salmon is on the grill, combine the salsa ingredients in a bowl and toss gently to combine.

Transfer the fillets to a platter, top each one with a spoonful of salsa, and pass the remaining salsa on the side.

GRILLED MUSSELS WITH MANGO CURRY SAUCE

Mussels are wonderful on the grill, not only because the smoky flavor really enlivens them, but also because they are self-timing: When they open, they're done. We like to complement that grill-ready aspect of these tasty mollusks by making the sauce for them in a pan set right on the grill. This is an ideal appetizer to serve to your guests while you're cooking the main course, since you never have to leave your place at the grill.

Serves 4 to 6 as an appetizer

THE INGREDIENTS

½ cup unsalted butter, softened
1 tablespoon good-quality curry powder
1 tablespoon peeled and minced fresh ginger
½ cup mango juice (or substitute equal parts orange juice
  and pineapple juice)
1 tablespoon minced fresh chile peppers of your choice
4lb (2kg) mussels (about 45–50), scrubbed and debearded
4 slices of good French bread, about 1in (2.5cm) thick
Juice of 2 limes (about ¼ cup)
¼ cup roughly chopped fresh cilantro
Kosher salt and freshly cracked black pepper to taste

Light a fire well over to one side of your grill (*see p31*), using enough coals to fill a shoebox. When the coals are all ignited, the flames have died down, and the temperature is hot (*see p34*), you're ready to cook.

Make the sauce: Put the butter, curry powder, and ginger in a shallow foil pan that is large enough to hold all the mussels and sturdy enough to withstand the heat of the fire. Place the pan on the grill near the fire—not directly over it—and cook for about 2 minutes, stirring a few times, until the butter is melted and the mixture is fragrant. Add the mango juice and chiles, let the sauce come to a simmer, then slide the pan to the side of the grill away from the fire.

Put the mussels directly on the grill grid on the hot side of the grill and cook until they pop open (6–8 minutes). Use tongs to transfer the mussels to the pan with the sauce as they are done. (Discard any that do not open.)

While the mussels are cooking, arrange the bread slices around the perimeter of the fire and cook until lightly toasted—about 2 minutes per side.

When all the mussels are in the pan, stir them around a bit to coat with the sauce and sprinkle with the lime juice, cilantro, and salt and pepper. Serve them right out of the pan, along with the toasted bread to soak up the juices.

ROLL-YOUR-OWN GRILLED SHRIMP TACOS WITH ANCHO CHILE SAUCE

For years, these Mexican-inspired tacos have been among the favorite dishes at Chris's East Coast Grill. Three reasons: People love shrimp, they love Mexican flavors, and—perhaps most importantly—they love putting together their own meal. So when you set up the shrimp taco bar in your backyard, you're going to be a very popular host.

Serves 4 as an appetizer

THE SHRIMP

1 lb (450g) medium-large shrimp (16–20 per pound), peeled, deveined, and tails removed

2 tablespoons olive oil

1 tablespoon chile powder

Salt and freshly cracked black pepper to taste

THE SAUCE

⅓ cup ancho chiles, steeped in hot water for 40 minutes, drained, and puréed in a blender

1 teaspoon ground cumin

Juice of 2 limes (about ¼ cup)

Kosher salt and freshly cracked black pepper to taste

THE GARNISHES

1 ripe but firm avocado, peeled, pitted, diced small, and lightly coated with fresh lemon juice

½ small red onion, peeled and thinly sliced

1 cup shredded green cabbage

¼ cup roughly chopped fresh cilantro

1 cup diced tomato

2 slices peeled fresh pineapple, about ½ in (1cm) thick

1 tablespoon olive oil

Salt and freshly cracked black pepper to taste

THE WRAPS

8 corn or flour tortillas, 6–8 in (15–20cm) across

Build a fire in your grill. When the coals are all ignited, the flames have died down, and the temperature is hot (*see p34*), you're ready to cook.

Put all the garnish ingredients except the pineapple, oil, and salt and pepper in separate small bowls, arrange the bowls on a platter, then cover and set aside until serving time. Combine the sauce ingredients in a small bowl.

Rub the pineapple slices with olive oil, sprinkle with salt and pepper, and grill until golden brown and slightly charred (3–4 minutes per side). Dice the pineapple, put it in a small serving bowl, and cover to keep warm.

Rub the shrimp with olive oil and sprinkle with the chile powder and plenty of salt and pepper. Put them on the grill directly over the coals and cook until just opaque throughout (3–4 minutes each side). To check for doneness, make a cut in one and peek in. Halve the shrimp if desired, put in a serving bowl, and cover loosely to keep warm.

Put the tortillas on the grill to toast briefly, flipping every 10 seconds or so, until they are soft and pliable (about 1 minute). Wrap the stack of warm tortillas in a large napkin or foil, and bring them to the table along with the shrimp, the sauce, and the platter of garnishes so your guests can "roll their own."

GRILLED SWORDFISH WITH DRIED TOMATO-HOMEMADE RAISIN RELISH

It's fun to make things at home that you usually buy at the store; the difference is amazing. Here we make raisins and dried tomatoes using the simple technique of letting the fruit (and, yes, tomatoes are fruits) sit in a low oven for up to 10 hours. You'll love the plush texture and clean flavors they bring to the relish, which is a beautiful complement to meaty grilled swordfish.

Serves 4

THE FISH

4 swordfish steaks, about 1in (2.5cm) thick, 8oz (225g) each
2 tablespoons olive oil
2 tablespoons coriander seeds, freshly cracked
Kosher salt and freshly cracked black pepper

THE RELISH

6 plum tomatoes, cored and cut in half
2 tablespoons olive oil
1 cup whole green grapes
¼ cup extra virgin olive oil
2 tablespoons roughly chopped fresh oregano
1 tablespoon dry sherry
1 teaspoon minced fresh garlic
Pinch red pepper flakes
Kosher salt and freshly cracked black pepper to taste

Dry the fruits for the relish: Preheat the oven to 200°F (110°C). Rub the tomato halves with the 2 tablespoons of regular olive oil and place them cut side up on a wire rack set over a baking sheet. Put the grapes on the rack beside the tomatoes, and place the baking sheet on the middle shelf of the oven. Remove the grapes when they resemble plump raisins (4–6 hours). Return the tomatoes to the oven and leave them until they are reduced in size by about one-quarter and shriveled on the outside but still tender and juicy inside (2–4 hours more). Cut each dried tomato half in half again.

Combine the dried grapes and tomatoes in a medium bowl along with the extra virgin olive oil, oregano, sherry, garlic, red pepper flakes, and salt and pepper and mix well.

Build a fire in your grill. When the coals are all ignited, the flames have died down, and the temperature is hot (*see p34*), you're ready to cook.

Rub the swordfish steaks with oil and sprinkle them generously with coriander, salt, and pepper, pressing gently to be sure the seasonings adhere. Put the fish on the grill directly over the coals and cook until it is just opaque throughout (5–7 minutes per side). To check for doneness, poke the fish with your finger to test its firmness (*see p37*); if you're unsure, cut into a steak at its thickest point to be sure it is just opaque all the way through.

Arrange the swordfish steaks on a serving platter, top each with a spoonful of relish, and pass the remaining relish on the side.

BLACK-AND-BLUE TUNA "HAWAIIAN STYLE" WITH QUICK CUCUMBER-SESAME RELISH

At one point in my rather aimless youth, I (Chris) spent some time surfing—and occasionally working in restaurant kitchens—in Lahaina on the Hawaiian island of Maui. I ate a lot of poke, a raw fish dish that is a traditional Hawaiian snack. This is a variation on that theme, in which we sear tuna hard on the outside, then mix it with traditional poke flavors. Because the fish spends only a short time over the flames, when you cut into it you'll get some sear and some raw in each bite—a great combination.

Serves 4 as an appetizer

THE FISH

3 tablespoons sesame seeds

1 hyper-fresh tuna steak, about 1lb (450g) in weight and about 2in (5cm) thick

2 tablespoons Asian sesame oil

2 tablespoons freshly cracked white pepper

2 tablespoons freshly cracked coriander seeds (or substitute 1 tablespoon ground coriander)

1 tablespoon kosher salt

3 scallions, including green tops, minced

THE RELISH

1 cucumber, peeled and seeded if desired, diced small

3 tablespoons Asian sesame oil

Juice of 1 lime (about 2 tablespoons)

2 tablespoons peeled and minced fresh ginger

1 tablespoon granulated sugar

Kosher salt to taste

Build a fire in your grill. When the coals are all ignited, the fire has died down, and the temperature is hot (*see p34*), you're ready to cook.

Meanwhile, on the stove top, toast the sesame seeds in a dry skillet over medium heat, shaking frequently to avoid burning, until they are fragrant and just a shade darker (3–5 minutes). Set them aside.

Combine the relish ingredients in a medium bowl; mix well and divide among 4 salad plates.

Cut the tuna steak into four 2in (5cm) cubes, and put them into a bowl. Drizzle the tuna with the sesame oil, add the pepper, coriander, and salt, and toss gently to coat. Place the tuna on the hottest part of the grill and sear until you have a dark brown, crispy crust on at least 2 sides (3–4 minutes per side). You're aiming for a dark, crusty exterior, and a cool, raw center.

Transfer the fish to a cutting board, slice it thin, and fan the slices out beside the cucumber relish on each plate. Garnish with the toasted sesame seeds and scallions and serve.

GRILLED LEMON-PEPPER MACKEREL
WITH TOMATO-GREEN OLIVE RELISH

Full-flavored, rich, and distinct, the mackerel is one of our favorite fish, with plenty of character to stand up to the grill flavor. The relish we serve with the mackerel here has Portuguese overtones, in tribute to the sardines we had on the beach in the Algarve many years ago (*see p96*), which convinced us of the virtues of grilling rich-flavored fish.

Serves 4

THE FISH

4 mackerel fillets, about 8oz (225g) each (or substitute fillets of bluefish, pompano, or salmon)
2 tablespoons olive oil

THE RUB

2 tablespoons freshly cracked black pepper
1 tablespoon finely minced lemon zest
½ teaspoon ground ginger
Kosher salt to taste

THE RELISH

1 tablespoon cumin seed (or 1½ teaspoons ground cumin)
2 ripe tomatoes, cored and diced large
½ cup roughly chopped pitted green olives
¼ cup extra virgin olive oil
¼ cup roughly chopped fresh parsley
¼ cup roughly chopped fresh mint
2 tablespoons drained capers
Kosher salt and freshly cracked black pepper

If using whole cumin seeds in the relish, toast them on the stove top in a skillet over medium-high heat until they are fragrant and just a shade darker (3–5 minutes). Set them aside.

Build a fire in your grill. When the coals are all ignited, the fire has died down, and the temperature is medium (*see p34*), you're ready to cook.

While the coals are heating up, make the relish: Combine the cumin, tomatoes, olives, olive oil, parsley, mint, and capers in a medium bowl and mix well. Season to taste with salt and pepper, and transfer to a serving dish.

Now make the rub: Combine the black pepper, lemon zest, ginger, and salt in a small bowl and mix well.

Rub the mackerel fillets all over with the olive oil and then coat with the spice rub, pressing gently to be sure it adheres. Put the fillets on the grill over the coals and cook until they are nicely seared on the outside and just opaque on the inside (4–6 minutes per side). To check for doneness, manipulate one of the fillets so you can see inside it at its thickest point to be sure it is just opaque all the way through.

Serve each fillet topped with a spoonful of relish, and pass the remaining relish on the side.

GRILLED CLAMS IN CHILE-BUTTER SAUCE

This is a variation on Clams Johnson, a dish invented in the late 1980s by our friend Steve Johnson, now the chef/owner of the Rendezvous restaurant in Cambridge, Massachusetts. We like digging clams along the Massachusetts coast, and this is a great way to cook them. Like mussels, they take well to the smoky flavor of the grill and have the added advantage of letting you know when they're cooked, because they pop open. You can also serve these over pasta, if you like.

Serves 4 as an appetizer

THE INGREDIENTS

½ cup unsalted butter, softened
½ cup white wine
1 tablespoon minced garlic
1 teaspoon red pepper flakes
32 littleneck clams, scrubbed
4 slices of good French bread, about 1in (2.5cm) thick
¼ cup roughly chopped fresh parsley
Kosher salt and freshly cracked black pepper to taste

Light a fire well over to one side of your grill, using enough coals to fill a shoebox. When the coals are all ignited, the flames have died down, and the temperature is hot (*see p34*), you're ready to cook.

Put the butter, wine, garlic, and red pepper flakes in a shallow foil pan that is large enough to hold all the clams in a single layer and sturdy enough to resist the heat of the fire. Place the pan on the grill near the fire, not directly over it, and cook for about 2 minutes, stirring a few times, until the butter is melted and the mixture is fragrant. Let the sauce come to a simmer, then slide the pan over to the side of the grill away from the fire.

Place the clams on the hot side of the grill, directly on the grill grate, and cook them until they pop open (8–10 minutes). Use tongs to transfer the clams to the pan containing the sauce as they are done. (Discard any clams that do not open.)

While the clams are cooking, arrange the bread slices around the perimeter of the fire and grill until lightly toasted (about 2 minutes per side).

When all the clams are in the pan, stir them around a bit to coat with the sauce, and sprinkle generously with parsley and salt and pepper. Serve them right out of the pan, along with the toasted bread to soak up the juices.

EXOTIC SPICE-GRILLED BLUEFISH
WITH MIRIN-MUSTARD SAUCE

The Japanese are, of course, masters of seafood, and have a particularly deft way with strong-flavored ingredients like eel and mackerel. Here we pair a sweet and pungent Japanese-style sauce with bluefish, another fish with a somewhat aggressive flavor. To add to the party, we coat the fish with a homemade five-spice powder before it goes over the flames. While you're at it, you might double or triple the quantities for the spice rub, just to have some extra on hand for rubbing on other fish for the grill.

Serves 4

THE FISH

4 bluefish fillets, about 8oz (225g) each
2 tablespoons Asian sesame oil
Kosher salt and freshly cracked black pepper

THE SPICE RUB

1 teaspoon ground ginger
1 teaspoon ground white pepper
1 teaspoon ground coriander
Pinch of ground cinnamon
Pinch of ground cardamom

THE SAUCE

¼ cup Dijon mustard
¼ cup mirin (sweet rice wine)
2 tablespoons rice vinegar
2 tablespoons Asian sesame oil
2 tablespoons minced scallions
Kosher salt and freshly cracked black pepper to taste

Build a fire in your grill. When the coals are all ignited, the fire has died down, and the temperature is medium (*see p34*), you're ready to cook.

Combine the spice rub ingredients in a small bowl and mix well.

Rub the fish fillets with sesame oil, sprinkle with salt and pepper, then coat them generously with the spice rub, pressing gently to be sure it adheres. Put the fillets on the grill over the coals, skin side up, and cook until just opaque all the way through (6–8 minutes per side). To check for doneness, poke the fish with your finger to test its firmness (*see p37*); if you're unsure, cut into one of the fillets at its thickest point to be sure it is just opaque all the way through.

While the fish cooks, make the sauce: Whisk the mustard, mirin, vinegar, sesame oil, and scallions together in a small bowl; season to taste with salt and pepper.

Serve the bluefish drizzled with mustard sauce, and pass any remaining sauce on the side.

SOUTHEAST ASIAN-STYLE GRILLED SHRIMP

Shrimp are a breeze on the grill—quick, easy, and very tasty. The main thing you have to do is be sure you don't overcook them; as soon as they are just opaque all the way through, take them off the fire. Here we combine them with a range of Southeast Asian flavors, including the classic herb trio of mint, basil, and cilantro, for a quick but superflavorful appetizer.

Serves 4 as an appetizer

THE INGREDIENTS

1lb (450g) extra-large shrimp (12 or less per pound,
   peeled and deveined, tails intact)

2 tablespoons olive oil

Kosher salt and freshly cracked white pepper

1 recipe Chile-Fish Sauce Condiment (*see p115*)

1 tablespoon roughly chopped fresh mint

1 tablespoon roughly chopped fresh Thai basil
   (or substitute Italian basil)

1 tablespoon roughly chopped fresh cilantro

Build a fire in your grill. When the coals are all ignited, the flames have died down, and the temperature is hot (*see p34*), you're ready to cook.

Rub the shrimp with oil, sprinkle generously with salt and white pepper, then put them on the grill directly over the coals and cook until they are just cooked through (3–4 minutes per side). To check for doneness, poke the shrimp with your finger to test their firmness (*see p37*); if you're unsure, make a cut in one of the shrimp at its thickest point to be sure it is just opaque all the way through.

Transfer the shrimp to a large bowl, add the Chile-Fish Sauce Condiment, and toss gently until the shrimp are thoroughly coated. Add the mint, basil, and cilantro, and toss again. Divide the shrimp among four plates and serve.

THINGS WITH WINGS

CHICKEN, THAT MOST EVERYDAY OF MODERN FOWL, TAKES ON A WHOLE NEW FLAVOR WHEN COOKED OVER THE SMOKY HEAT OF A CHARCOAL FIRE. SLIGHTLY MORE EXOTIC BIRDS, FROM DUCK TO QUAIL TO SQUAB, ALSO COME INTO THEIR OWN OVER THE GRILL. MATCHED WITH FLAVORS FROM AROUND THE WORLD, THEY'RE IRRESISTIBLE.

GRILLED ORANGE CHICKEN BREAST
WITH CHUNKY GINGER-PLUM SAUCE

We love combining fruit and meat, and this approach works very well with poultry, too. We leave the plums in this sauce rather chunky, because it creates more textural contrast between the interior and exterior of the fruit; but for a somewhat more elegant sauce, you can also just purée the mixture once it's cooked. If good-quality plums aren't available, feel free to substitute apricots, peaches, or even mangoes.

Serves 4

THE CHICKEN

4 boneless skin-on chicken breasts, 10–12oz (300–350g) each
3 tablespoons olive oil
Kosher salt and freshly cracked black pepper
¼ cup finely minced orange zest

THE SAUCE

2 tablespoons olive oil
1 medium red onion, peeled and diced small
3 ripe plums, pitted and quartered
1 tablespoon peeled and minced fresh ginger
Juice of 1 lemon (about ¼ cup)
⅓ cup roughly chopped fresh parsley
Kosher salt and freshly cracked black pepper to taste

Build a fire in your grill. When the coals are all ignited, the flames have died down, and the temperature is medium (see p34), you're ready to cook.

Rub the chicken breasts with the oil and sprinkle them generously with salt and pepper and the orange zest, pressing gently so it adheres. Put the chicken on the grill directly over the coals, skin side down, and cook, turning once, until they are opaque all the way through (7–9 minutes per side). To check for doneness, poke the chicken with your finger to test its firmness (see p37); if you're unsure, make a small cut in the thickest part of one piece to be sure there is no pinkness in the center.

While the chicken is cooking, make the sauce: On the stove top, heat the oil in a large sauté pan over medium-high heat until hot but not smoking. Add the onions and sauté, stirring occasionally, until golden brown (11–13 minutes). Add the plums and ginger and cook, stirring frequently, for another 3 minutes, or until the plums are tender but not mushy. Remove from the heat, stir in the lemon juice and parsley, and add salt and pepper to taste.

Serve the chicken hot, with a spoonful of plum sauce on each piece. Pass the remaining sauce on the side.

GRILLED DUCK BREAST WITH ORANGE-CARDAMOM GLAZE

Here's a twist on the French classic duck à l'orange, but a lot easier and a little more exotic, with subtly aromatic cardamom and the subdued bite of ginger added to the sweet-tart of the orange. This is a great dish to serve when you want to seem a little fancy but don't want to spend a whole lot of time cooking.

Serves 4

THE DUCK

4 boneless duck breasts, 10–12oz (300–350g) each, with most of the fat removed
2 tablespoons olive oil
Kosher salt and freshly cracked black pepper

THE GLAZE

1 cup orange juice
1 cup red wine
2 tablespoons peeled and minced fresh ginger
1 tablespoon finely minced orange zest
2 green cardamom pods, lightly cracked
2 tablespoons dark brown sugar
Kosher salt and freshly cracked black pepper to taste

Build a fire in your grill. When the coals are all ignited, the flames have died down, and the temperature is medium (*see p34*), you're ready to cook.

Combine the glaze ingredients in a small saucepan and bring to a boil on the stove top over medium heat, stirring occasionally. Adjust the heat so the mixture just simmers gently, and cook until it has been reduced to about ⅔ cup (25–30 minutes). Remove from the heat and set it aside.

Rub the duck breasts with the oil, sprinkle them generously with salt and pepper, and arrange them skin side down on the grill, off to the edge of the coals. Cook the duck slowly, allowing the fat to drip off at an even pace and giving the skin time to crisp (6–8 minutes per side). If fat drips into the fire and causes flare-ups, move the duck breasts so they are not directly over the flames. During the last minute of cooking, brush them liberally with the glaze. When the duck is nicely browned, check for doneness by poking the meat with your finger to test its firmness (*see p37*); if you're unsure, make a small cut in the thickest part of one breast; it should be slightly less done than you like (we prefer them medium-rare).

Serve, passing the remaining glaze on the side.

FLAVOR FOOTPRINT INDIA

From the lentil and rice dishes of Gujarat to the tandoor cooking of the Punjab and the fiery lamb dishes of Andhra Pradesh, the cuisines of India are at least as varied as those of Europe. All, however, are characterized by the expert use of a wide variety of spices, very often used whole, and frequently combined into signature spice mixes called masalas. The five recipes here provide a quick primer on the way spices can add powerful excitement to everyday food without much effort.

All-Purpose Indian Masala Rub
Makes about 1 cup

This complex dry spice rub is excellent rubbed on steaks, chops of any variety, or chicken before grilling.

¼ cup coriander seeds
2 tablespoons cumin seeds
2 tablespoons yellow mustard seeds
2 tablespoons fennel seeds
2 tablespoons white peppercorns
2 small dried red chiles
2 tablespoons kosher salt
1 tablespoon ground ginger
1 tablespoon ground turmeric

Combine the coriander seeds, cumin seeds, mustard seeds, fennel seeds, peppercorns, and chiles in a dry skillet over medium-high heat and toast until fragrant (3–4 minutes), shaking the pan frequently. Remove from the heat and cool to room temperature. Transfer to a spice mill or clean coffee grinder, add the salt, ginger, and turmeric, and grind to a coarse powder. Stored in an airtight container and kept in a cool, dark place, this dry rub will last for months.

Curry-Mint Paste
Makes just over 1 cup

Use this as a last-minute rub before lamb, chicken, or pork go on the grill, or as a quick marinade (up to 3 hours before cooking).

½ cup minced fresh mint leaves
¼ cup minced fresh cilantro leaves
2 tablespoons curry powder
2 tablespoons vegetable oil
1 tablespoon minced fresh ginger
1 tablespoon kosher salt

Combine all the ingredients in a small bowl or, if you prefer a finer paste, mash in a mortar and pestle. This will last, covered and refrigerated, for 2–3 days.

All-Purpose Indian Masala Rub

Fresh Coconut Condiment
Makes about 1¼ cups

This is perfect with fish fillets or chicken breasts.

¾ cup grated fresh coconut
Juice of 2 limes (about ¼ cup)
¼ cup roughly chopped fresh cilantro
2 tablespoons roughly chopped fresh green chile peppers
   of your choice
1 tablespoon peeled and minced fresh ginger
1 teaspoon granulated sugar
Kosher salt and freshly cracked black pepper to taste

Combine all the ingredients in a small bowl and mix well. This condiment will keep, covered and refrigerated, for 2–3 days.

Spicy Tomato Relish
Makes about 2 cups

Put out a bowl of this whenever you are serving smaller pieces of fish, chicken, or pork.

1 ripe tomato, cored and diced small
⅓ cup diced cucumber
⅓ cup roughly chopped fresh cilantro
Juice of 1 lemon (about ¼ cup)
2 tablespoons minced fresh green chiles of your choice
1 tablespoon brown mustard seeds
1 teaspoon ground cumin
Kosher salt and freshly cracked black pepper to taste

Combine all the ingredients in a medium bowl and mix well. This relish will keep, covered and refrigerated, for 3–4 days.

SIGNATURE INGREDIENTS/TOP ROW (LEFT TO RIGHT) Turmeric, cardamom, fennel seeds, mustard seeds; **SECOND ROW** Lime, cumin seeds, ginger, mint; **THIRD ROW** Saffron, tamarind, coconut, fenugreek; **BOTTOM ROW** Cilantro, chiles, coriander seed, garlic.

Dried Apricot Chutney
Makes about 2 cups

This is great to make in the winter, when it's hard to find good-quality fresh fruit. Try it with pork, lamb, or in fact any roasted meat.

2 tablespoons olive oil
½ small red onion, peeled and diced small
1 cup roughly chopped dried apricots
1 tablespoon peeled and minced fresh ginger
1 tablespoon minced fresh chile pepper of your choice
¼ cup fresh orange juice
¼ cup red wine vinegar
Juice of 1 lime (about 2 tablespoons)
Kosher salt and freshly cracked black pepper to taste

Heat the oil in a sauté pan over medium-high heat until hot but not smoking. Add the onions and sauté, stirring occasionally, until transparent (7–9 minutes). Add the apricots, ginger, and chile, and cook, stirring frequently, until fragrant (about 2 minutes more). Add the orange juice and vinegar and mix well. Bring to a simmer, adjust the heat to low, and cook gently, stirring frequently, until the mixture thickens—about 10 minutes. Remove from the heat and let cool slightly. Add the lime juice and mix well. This chutney will keep, covered and refrigerated, for about a week.

Spicy Tomato Relish

GRILLED QUAIL WITH ANCHO-PEANUT MOLE

We love quail, not only because they're delicious but also because you can pick them up and eat them with your fingers even in polite company. They are also great for grilling, since they cook quickly and the sear and smoke complements the rather delicate flavor of the bird. We like to pair them with rather strongly flavored sauces—like those in the Mexican-inspired mole made with anchos (dried poblano chiles) that accompanies them here.

Serves 8 as an appetizer, 4 as a main course

THE QUAIL

8 quail, either semi-boneless or butterflied with the backbone removed

2 tablespoons olive oil

Kosher salt and freshly cracked black pepper

¼ cup roughly chopped fresh cilantro

Juice of 1 lime (about 2 tablespoons)

THE MOLE

4 ancho chiles, seeded and stemmed

3 tablespoons olive oil

1 small red onion, peeled and diced small

¼ cup roasted unsalted peanuts

2 tablespoons minced fresh garlic

½ a baseball-sized tomato, cored and chopped (about ½ cup)

⅓ cup distilled white vinegar

2 tablespoons orange juice

1 teaspoon ground cumin

1 teaspoon ground coriander

Pinch of cinnamon

Kosher salt and freshly cracked black pepper to taste

Build a fire in your grill. When the coals are all ignited, the flames have died down, and the temperature is medium-hot (*see p34*), you're ready to cook.

For the mole: On the stove top, toast the chiles in a small skillet over medium heat until fragrant (2–3 minutes); place in a small bowl and cover with boiling water. Let them soak for 40 minutes to rehydrate them, then drain.

Heat the oil in a sauté pan or skillet over medium-high heat until hot but not smoking. Add the onion and sauté, stirring occasionally, until transparent (7–9 minutes). Add the peanuts and garlic and sauté, stirring frequently, until fragrant, about 2 minutes more. Stir in the chiles and the tomato, vinegar, orange juice, cumin, coriander, cinnamon, and salt and pepper. Bring to a simmer and cook, stirring occasionally, for 15 minutes. Set aside to cool slightly, then transfer to a blender or food processor and purée. Return the mole to the sauté pan.

Rub the quails with oil, sprinkle them generously with salt and pepper, then put them on the grill directly over the coals and cook until there is no more than a hint of pink near the bone when you cut into them (4–6 minutes per side). Transfer the quail to a large, shallow serving bowl and cover loosely to keep warm.

Reheat the mole, thinning with water if necessary. Pour the sauce over the quail, turning to coat; sprinkle with the cilantro and lime juice, and serve.

GRILLED BONE-IN CHICKEN BREASTS
WITH GRILLED APPLES AND GOLDEN RAISIN VINAIGRETTE

This simple late summer/early fall recipe takes advantage of grilled apples—delicious and easy, but still unusual enough in most cooks' repertoires to seem somewhat exotic. Granny Smith apples work well, but if you have a local apple that is firm and a little tart, then use it.

Serves 4

THE CHICKEN

4 bone-in, skin-on split chicken breasts, 10–12oz (300–350g) each

2 tablespoons vegetable oil

Kosher salt and freshly cracked black pepper

THE APPLES

2 Granny Smith or other green apples, halved through the stem and cored

1 tablespoon vegetable oil

Kosher salt and freshly cracked black pepper to taste

THE VINAIGRETTE

⅓ cup extra virgin olive oil

¼ cup balsamic vinegar

¼ cup golden raisins, finely chopped

2 tablespoons minced fresh sage

1 teaspoon dark brown sugar

Build a multilevel fire in your grill (*see p31*). When the coals are all ignited, the fire has died down, and the temperature is medium (*see p34*), you're ready to cook.

Rub the chicken breasts with vegetable oil, sprinkle generously with salt and pepper, and place them skin side down on the hottest part of the grill. Cook until the skin is very brown and crisp (about 4 minutes); flip them over and cook on the other side for about 4 minutes more. To finish, move the breasts to the cooler side of the grill, skin side down, and cover them with an inverted foil pan until they are completely opaque inside but not dried out (10–12 minutes more). To check for doneness, poke the meat with your finger to test its firmness (*see p37*); if you're unsure, cut into the thickest part of the largest breast and check to be sure it is opaque all the way through, with no redness near the bone.

While the chicken is cooking, make the vinaigrette: Combine the olive oil, vinegar, raisins, sage, and brown sugar in a bowl large enough to hold at least one of the chicken breasts, whisking until the sugar dissolves. Set aside.

As soon as you move the chicken to the cooler side of the grill, rub the apple halves with vegetable oil, sprinkle them generously with salt and pepper, and arrange them, cut side down, beside the chicken. Cook the apples until the cut sides are golden brown (about 5 minutes).

As the chicken breasts are done, dunk them one at a time in the bowl of vinaigrette, then transfer to a serving platter. Arrange the apples around the chicken, drizzle the remaining vinaigrette over all, and serve.

CHILE-GARLIC-RUBBED GRILLED CHICKEN BREAST WITH LEMONGRASS-GINGER SLAW

If you're pressed for time, you can always make this delicious spice-rubbed chicken without the slaw. But the slaw is a great, subtle complement to the robust flavor of the chicken, and the unique aromatic taste of the lemongrass is worth the effort it takes to extract and chop the soft inner core.

Serves 4

THE CHICKEN

3 tablespoons Asian sesame oil

2 tablespoons minced fresh garlic

2 tablespoons minced fresh chile pepper of your choice

2 tablespoons kosher salt

2 tablespoons freshly cracked black pepper

4 boneless, skin-on full chicken breasts, 10–12oz (300–350g) each

THE SLAW

⅓ cup rice wine vinegar

3 tablespoons soy sauce

1 tablespoon Asian sesame oil

2 tablespoons peeled and minced fresh ginger

2 stalks lemongrass, minced (use the tender, inner portion of the bottom third only)

2 tablespoons roughly chopped fresh Thai basil (or substitute regular basil)

Juice of 1 lime (about 2 tablespoons)

2 tablespoons granulated sugar

Kosher salt and freshly cracked black pepper to taste

½ small head Napa cabbage, cut crosswise into thin strips (about 2 cups)

Build a fire in your grill. When the coals are all ignited, the flames have died down, and the temperature is medium (*see p34*), you're ready to cook.

Combine the sesame oil, garlic, chiles, salt, and pepper in a small bowl and mix well. Rub the chicken breasts with the sesame mixture, place them on the grill, skin side down, and cook, turning once, until they are opaque all the way through (7–9 minutes per side). To check for doneness, poke the chicken with your finger to test its firmness (*see p37*); if you're unsure, make a small cut in the thickest part of the largest breast to be sure that it is opaque all the way through.

While the chicken is on the grill, combine all of the slaw ingredients except the cabbage in a small bowl and whisk until well blended. Put the cabbage in a large bowl, add enough dressing to just moisten it, and toss until the cabbage is well coated. Divide the slaw among 4 plates.

When the chicken is done, transfer the breasts to a carving board and slice them crosswise into strips. Fan the chicken over the slaw on each plate, and drizzle with any remaining dressing.

GRILLED SUPER-FIERY WEST INDIAN CHICKEN BREASTS WITH SOUR ORANGE MOJO

In this tribute to the jerk masters of Jamaica's Boston Bay (*see also p162*), a flavorful spice paste forms a super-hot and spicy crust on the outside of tender chicken breasts. It's an ideal dish if you like chicken, but are tired of the usual ways of preparing it. The sourness of the orange mojo provides just the right complement to the fiery chicken; it's also good served alongside just about any other kind of grilled fowl.

Serves 4

THE CHICKEN

4 boneless, skinless full chicken breasts, 10–12oz (300–350g) each

⅓ cup yellow mustard

4 Scotch bonnet chile peppers, stemmed

1 tablespoon peeled and minced fresh ginger

1 tablespoon good-quality curry powder

¼ cup roughly chopped scallions, white and green parts

Kosher salt and freshly cracked black pepper to taste

THE MOJO

Juice of 2 oranges (about 1 cup)

⅓ cup distilled white vinegar

⅓ cup olive oil

2 tablespoons roughly chopped fresh oregano

1 tablespoon minced fresh garlic

1 tablespoon minced fresh chili pepper of your choice

Kosher salt and freshly cracked black pepper to taste

Place the chicken breasts in a large, shallow bowl. Combine the mustard, chiles, ginger, curry powder, scallions, and salt and pepper in a blender or food processor and purée; pour over the chicken, turning each piece to coat. Cover and refrigerate for 1 hour, turning once or twice if you remember.

While the chicken marinates, build a fire in your grill. When the coals are all ignited, the flames have died down, and the temperature is medium (*see p34*), you're ready to cook.

Combine all the mojo ingredients in a medium bowl, mix well, and set aside.

Place the chicken breasts on the grill directly over the coals and cook, turning once, until they are opaque all the way through (7–9 minutes per side). To check for doneness, poke the chicken with your finger to test its firmness (*see p37*); if you're unsure, make a small cut in the thickest part of the largest breast to be sure that it is opaque all the way through.

To serve, arrange the chicken breasts on a serving platter and spoon the mojo over them.

GRILLED CHICKEN DRUMSTICKS
WITH ORANGES AND GREEN OLIVES

We think chicken drumsticks are a seriously underrated food: They have much more flavor than the more popular chicken breasts, you can eat them with your fingers, and they are usually inexpensive. For a bit of exotic allure that will hopefully improve their image, we serve them with a Moroccan-inspired mixture of oranges and olives enlivened with lemon juice, garlic, and hot peppers.

Serves 4

THE INGREDIENTS

2 large oranges
½ cup pitted green olives
Juice of 1½ lemons (about ⅓ cup)
¼ cup extra virgin olive oil
1 teaspoon minced fresh garlic
1 teaspoon red pepper flakes
Kosher salt and freshly cracked black pepper
8 chicken drumsticks

Build a fire in your grill. When the coals are all ignited, the flames have died down, and the temperature is medium-low (*see p34*), you're ready to cook.

Use a vegetable peeler to remove the zest from both oranges. Mince the zest and set it aside. (You should have about 2 tablespoons of zest.) With a sharp knife, remove and discard all of the white pith from the oranges. Working over a medium-size bowl to catch the juice, cut between the section membranes of each orange to remove each section whole, taking care to remove any seeds. Add the sections to the juice together with the olives, lemon juice, olive oil, reserved zest, garlic, red pepper flakes, and salt and pepper to taste; mix well and set aside.

Sprinkle the drumsticks generously with salt and pepper, then place them on the grill directly over the coals and cook for 12–14 minutes, rolling them around to ensure even browning. To check for doneness, poke the meat with your finger to test its firmness (*see p37*); if you're unsure, cut into the thickest part of the largest drumstick to be sure it's opaque all the way through, with no redness near the bone.

Arrange the drumsticks on a platter and spoon the orange-olive mixture over and around them.

JAMAICA: FEELING THE HEAT

After I (Chris) graduated from culinary school, I ran fairly quickly through a number of food industry jobs—private chef on a yacht that rarely left harbor, line cook at a resort in Hawaii, sous-chef at a large hotel in Boston....

I learned something from each of them, but none of them fired my imagination. So eventually I decided to do what any sensible young man would do—quit my job and embark on an epic surfing trip through the Caribbean and South and Central America. It was perhaps the best decision of my life, because it was on this trip that my formal training and my love of intensely flavored, casual food came together. About a third of the way through the trip, I was lucky enough to spend a series of languorous afternoons (because surfers are nothing if not languorous when the surf isn't up) on the northern coast of Jamaica, near Boston Bay. As any aficionado knows, this is the original home of "jerk" cooking, a unique technique originally developed by runaway slaves called maroons. Jerk involves coating meat (most often chicken or pork) with a spice paste featuring the incendiary Scotch bonnet chile pepper, which is among the very hottest in the world but also has a distinctly floral, aromatic flavor. Once the paste is applied, the food is slowly cooked over a smoky fire, usually fueled by pimento wood. The guys who hang out around the pits cooking jerk may be the very definition of laid-back, but the food they produce is anything but—it's a smoke-infused, aromatic, blisteringly hot treat. I quickly became addicted. Plus, from watching these guys and eating their food, I learned the virtues of spice pastes. Because they include fresh ingredients such as garlic and fresh chiles, these pastes have even more dynamic flavors than the dry spice rubs I had already begun using. And, really, you can't ask more than that—lazy days in the sun, great food, and a culinary lesson you use for the rest of your life.

JERK WINGS FROM HELL

These super-fiery wings, powered by the outrageous Scotch bonnet chile pepper, are one of the most popular snacks for the macho line cooks at Chris's East Coast Grill. When these wings come fresh off the grill, we can practically guarantee you will go for them, even if you're not a chile aficionado.

Serves 4 as an appetizer

2lb (900g) chicken wings
2 tablespoons olive oil
Kosher salt and freshly cracked black pepper
¼ cup distilled white vinegar
1 large fresh Scotch bonnet chile pepper, minced (about 2 tablespoons)
2 tablespoons yellow mustard
2 tablespoons dried oregano
Kosher salt and freshly cracked black pepper to taste
2 tablespoons minced fresh scallion
1 lime, halved

Build a fire in your grill. When the coals are all ignited, the flames have died down, and the temperature is medium (*see p34*), you're ready to cook.

Cut each wing into 3 sections. Discard the wing tips or save them for stock.

Rub the wing pieces with the oil, sprinkle them generously with salt and pepper, then put them on the grill directly over the coals and cook, rolling them around regularly to be sure they cook evenly, until they are golden brown (10–15 minutes). To check for doneness, cut into one to make sure there is no redness near the bone.

While the wings are cooking, combine the vinegar, chile, mustard, oregano, and salt and pepper in a bowl large enough to hold all of the wings and mix well.

As the wings come off the grill, add them to the bowl of sauce, turning to coat. Sprinkle the wings with the scallions, squeeze on the lime juice, and serve them right out of the bowl.

HONEY- AND GINGER-GLAZED SQUAB
WITH SMOKY FIGS, BACON, AND POMEGRANATE

Game birds are great on the grill because they respond very well to high-heat cooking. This is particularly true of the young, plump pigeons known as squab, which to us have many of the flavor characteristics of beef, including being best served rare.

Serves 4

THE SQUAB

Juice of 1 lemon (about ¼ cup)
¼ cup olive oil
2 tablespoons peeled and minced fresh ginger
2 tablespoons freshly cracked coriander seeds
1 tablespoon minced garlic
4 medium-sized squab, butterflied
Kosher salt and freshly cracked black pepper

THE GLAZE

¼ cup honey
2 tablespoons roughly chopped fresh mint
1 tablespoon peeled and minced fresh ginger
1 tablespoon fresh lemon juice
1 teaspoon red pepper flakes

THE GARNISHES

6 slices thick bacon, diced large
5 fresh figs, halved lengthwise
1 tablespoon olive oil
Kosher salt and freshly cracked black pepper
⅓ cup pomegranate seeds
¼ cup roughly chopped fresh parsley

Combine the lemon juice, olive oil, ginger, coriander, and garlic in a medium bowl and mix well. Sprinkle the squab generously with salt and pepper, and arrange them in a single layer in a shallow glass baking dish. Pour the marinade over the birds, turning to coat on all sides. Cover with plastic wrap and refrigerate for at least 1 and up to 3 hours.

Cook the bacon over medium heat in a sauté pan until crisp (6–8 minutes). Transfer to paper towels to drain.

Rub the figs with olive oil and sprinkle generously with salt and pepper.

Make the glaze: Combine the honey, mint, ginger, lemon juice, and red pepper flakes in a small bowl, and mix well.

Build a multilevel fire in your grill (*see p31*). When the coals are all ignited, the flames have died down, and the temperature is medium-hot (*see p34*), you're ready to cook.

Arrange the squab on the hot side of the grill and cook until just cooked through (5–7 minutes per side). To check for doneness, cut into the thickest part of one of the thighs; the juices should run clear, and there should be only a hint of pink near the bone. When the squab are done, move them to the cooler side of the grill. Brush generously with the glaze, and let sit for 2 minutes more on each side. (Be careful not to burn the glaze.)

When you move the squab, put the figs on the hot side of the grill, cut side down. Cook until just browned (2–3 minutes). Arrange the squab and figs on a platter. Scatter the bacon, pomegranate seeds, and parsley over all.

SMOKE-ROASTED CHICKEN THIGHS
WITH MAPLE BARBECUE SAUCE

We're big fans of chicken thighs because they're very tasty and easy to prepare, and they have just enough fat to stay moist on the grill. This is a deliciously sweet, sticky, old-school treatment most often used with wings, but we like it even better with thighs. These are not only great hot off the grill (*see overleaf*), but when they're cold, too, making them perfect for picnics.

Serves 4

THE CHICKEN

8 large, bone-in chicken thighs, about
   8oz (225g) each

THE SPICE RUB

2 tablespoons ground coriander
2 tablespoons paprika
2 tablespoons ground cumin
2 tablespoons dark brown sugar
2 tablespoons freshly cracked black pepper
1 tablespoon kosher salt

THE BARBECUE SAUCE

¾ cup ketchup
⅓ cup maple syrup
Juice of 1 lemon (about ¼ cup)

Light a fire well over to one side of your grill, using enough coals to fill a large shoebox. When the fire has died down and the coals are covered with white ash, you're ready to cook.

Combine the spice rub ingredients in a small bowl and mix well.

Coat the thighs generously with the spice rub, pressing gently to be sure it adheres, then arrange them, skin side down, on the side of the grill away from the coals, being careful that none of the meat is directly over the coals. Put the lid on the grill with the vents open one-quarter of the way and cook for about 1 hour, adding a handful of fresh charcoal and flipping the thighs over after 30 minutes. To check for doneness, cut into one of the thighs at its thickest point; there should be no redness near the bone.

While the chicken is on the grill, combine the ketchup, maple syrup, and lemon juice in a small bowl and mix well. Baste the chicken with the sauce during the last 10 minutes of cooking, and serve the remaining sauce along with the smoked thighs.

PORT-GLAZED GRILLED PHEASANT BREASTS

When we were growing up, the *ne plus ultra* of fine dining was breast of pheasant "under glass." Unfortunately, that rather silly treatment gave a bad name to a perfectly good piece of fowl. We try to resurrect its reputation here by serving it with a take on the traditional Cumberland sauce, adapted for ease and grilling pleasure.

Serves 4 to 6

THE PHEASANT

6 boneless pheasant breasts, 5–6oz (140–175g) each
2 tablespoons olive oil
Kosher salt and freshly cracked black pepper
3 tablespoons roughly chopped fresh thyme leaves

THE GLAZE

½ cup port
½ cup red currant jelly
1 tablespoon finely minced orange zest
Kosher salt and freshly cracked black pepper to taste

Build a fire in your grill. When the coals are all ignited, the flames have died down, and the temperature is medium (*see p34*), you're ready to cook.

Make the glaze: Combine the port, red currant jelly, zest, and salt and pepper in a small saucepan and, on the stove top, bring it to a simmer over medium heat, whisking until the jelly melts. Adjust the heat so the glaze simmers gently and cook until it has reduced by half and has a sticky consistency (25–30 minutes). Transfer the glaze to a small bowl and set it aside.

Rub the pheasant breasts with the olive oil, sprinkle them generously with salt and pepper, and pat the thyme onto them. Put them on the grill directly over the coals and cook for 6–8 minutes per side, brushing with the glaze for the last 30 seconds of cooking. To check for doneness, poke the meat with your finger to test its firmness (*see p37*); if you're unsure, cut into one to be sure that there is just a hint of pink at the center. Serve, passing the remaining glaze on the side.

GRILLED DEVILED GAME HENS
WITH CARAMELIZED ONIONS, PANCETTA, AND SAGE

This is our modernized version of the approach that the great 19th-century French chef Auguste Escoffier used with grilled food, which involves lots of breadcrumbs. Today it's quite unusual, but it's still very delicious. And game hens are fun to serve because it seems indulgent—almost decadent—when each person gets a whole bird.

Serves 4

Onion, pancetta, and sage garnish

THE HENS

4 Rock Cornish game hens, about 1½lb (675g) each, butterflied with backbone removed

Kosher salt and freshly cracked black pepper

THE BREADCRUMB COATING

⅓ cup wholegrain mustard

1 tablespoon Worcestershire sauce

1 tablespoon Tabasco

½ cup fresh breadcrumbs

2 tablespoons roughly chopped fresh parsley

1 tablespoon minced fresh garlic

Kosher salt and freshly cracked black pepper to taste

THE GARNISH

8oz (225g) pancetta, diced small (or substitute bacon)

2 red onions, peeled and sliced thin

Kosher salt and freshly cracked black pepper to taste

1 tablespoon roughly chopped fresh sage

Build a multilevel fire in your grill (*see p31*). When the coals are all ignited, the fire has died down, and the temperature is medium (*see p34*), you're ready to cook.

Sprinkle the hens generously with salt and pepper, place them skin side down on the hotter side of the grill, and cook until the skin is nicely browned (about 15 minutes). (If the hens start to darken too quickly, move them to the cooler side of the grill for the remainder of the 15 minutes.) Flip the hens over and cook until the other side is also brown and crisp (about 15 minutes more). To check for doneness, cut into one of the thighs, or where the wing meets the breast; the meat should be opaque throughout, with no pink near the bone.

While the hens are on the grill, cook the pancetta on the stove top in a large sauté pan over medium-low heat, stirring frequently, until it is crisp and brown (about 7 minutes). Transfer the pancetta to paper towels to drain, and discard all but 2 tablespoons of the rendered fat in the pan. Add the onions to the pan, season with salt and pepper, and sauté, stirring occasionally, until they are well caramelized (20–30 minutes). Add the sage during the last minute or two of cooking. Remove the pan from the heat.

Combine the mustard, Worcestershire sauce, and Tabasco in a small bowl and mix well. In another bowl, combine the breadcrumbs, parsley, garlic, and salt and pepper and toss until evenly mixed.

When the hens are just done, move them to the cooler side of the grill, slather them with the mustard mixture, and sprinkle them generously with the breadcrumbs, pressing gently to be sure they adhere. Leave the hens on the grill for another minute or two to toast the crumbs, then transfer them to a serving platter. Top each with some of the caramelized onions, sprinkle with the reserved pancetta, and serve.

Breadcrumb coating

SPICY GRILLED CHICKEN WINGS

Among the many virtues of chicken wings, perhaps the best of all is the very high ratio of crispy, super-flavorful skin to meat. To take advantage of this, we toss the wings with a spicy herb mixture right after they come off the grill, so the skin gets nicely coated. You probably already know this, but these make an excellent snack to serve when you have friends over to watch the big game.

Serves 4

THE WINGS

3lb (1.5kg) chicken wings

3 tablespoons olive oil

2 tablespoons smoked paprika *picante* (hot) (preferably the Spanish *pimentón de La Vera*)

Kosher salt and freshly cracked black pepper

THE DRESSING

¼ cup extra virgin olive oil

Juice of 1 lemon (about ¼ cup)

¼ cup roughly chopped fresh herbs: any combination of parsley, sage, rosemary, thyme, and oregano

2 tablespoons dry sherry

1 tablespoon minced fresh garlic

1 tablespoon red pepper flakes

Kosher salt and freshly cracked black pepper to taste

Build a fire in your grill. When the coals are all ignited, the flames have died down, and the temperature is medium (*see p34*), you're ready to cook.

Cut each wing into 3 sections. Discard the wing tips or save them for stock.

Rub the wing pieces with oil, sprinkle them with smoked paprika, salt, and pepper, then put them on the grill directly over the coals and cook, turning occasionally, until they are golden brown (10–15 minutes). To check for doneness, cut into one to make sure there is no redness near the bone.

While the wings are on the grill, combine the olive oil, lemon juice, fresh herbs, sherry, garlic, red pepper flakes, and salt and pepper in a bowl large enough to hold all of the wings; mix well.

As the wings come off the grill, add them to the bowl, turning to coat with the dressing. Serve the wings hot, right out of the bowl, with plenty of paper napkins.

PUT A LID ON IT

THERE'S NOTHING WE LIKE BETTER THAN RELAXING WITH FRIENDS, HAVING A COUPLE OF COLD ONES, WHILE SOMETHING DELICIOUS IS QUIETLY SOAKING UP THE SMOKY FLAVORS OF THE FIRE. IT'S THE EPITOME OF OUR FAVORITE FOOD MANTRA: "WORK SMARTER, NOT HARDER." EVEN BETTER—THE RESULTS ARE FANTASTIC.

TEXAS-STYLE SLOW BEEF BRISKET
WITH SPICY BARBECUE SAUCE

In Texas, beef brisket is the barbecue of choice. It is perhaps the ultimate example of taking a tough, gnarly piece of meat and transforming it into a super-tender delicacy through long, slow cooking. As with the pulled pork barbecue of North Carolina (*see pp196–9*), the preferred method is to make a night of it, putting the brisket on in the early evening and letting it cook until daylight. But this also makes a very good pastime for a lazy Saturday, a great way to spend time hanging out with friends then ending the day with a spectacularly delicious meal. The sauce, which has a little kick to it, can be made up to a week in advance, and then kept covered and refrigerated.

Serves 8 to 10

THE MEAT

1 beef brisket, 10–12lb (4.5–5.5kg)
3 tablespoons olive oil
¼ cup kosher salt
¼ cup freshly cracked black pepper

THE SAUCE

⅔ cup ketchup
½ cup cider vinegar
¼ cup dark brown sugar
2 tablespoons hot sauce of your choice
1 teaspoon ground cumin
1 teaspoon paprika
1 teaspoon kosher salt
1 teaspoon freshly cracked black pepper

Light a fire well over to one side of your grill, using enough coals to fill a large shoebox.

Rub the brisket with the oil and coat it evenly with salt and pepper, pressing gently to make sure it adheres.

When the fire has died down and the coals are covered with white ash, place the brisket on the side of the grill away from the coals, being careful that none of the meat is directly over the coals. Put the lid on the grill with the vents open one-quarter of the way and cook, adding a handful of fresh charcoal every 30 minutes or so, for 8–10 hours. To test for doneness, stick a big fork in the meat and try to lift it up—if it falls off the fork, it's done.

While the beef is on the grill, make the sauce: Combine the sauce ingredients in a small saucepan and mix well. On the stove top over medium heat, bring the mixture to a simmer and cook for 5 minutes to blend the flavors, then remove from the heat and transfer to a serving bowl.

To serve, slice the brisket thinly across the grain, and pass the barbecue sauce on the side.

SUPER-HOT JERK PORK SHOULDER
WITH SPICED PINEAPPLE CHUTNEY

Over the past few years, jerk has become one of the most widely interpreted (and misinterpreted) cooking methods in the world. This pork shoulder, which we accompany with a spicy chutney that also features the flavors of Jamaica, may not be fully authentic, but it's pretty close. Note that the meat may need anywhere up to 8 hours to cook.

Serves 8

THE MEAT

1 boneless pork butt or other boneless pork shoulder roast, about 5lb (2.25kg)

Kosher salt and freshly cracked black pepper

THE CHUTNEY

2 tablespoons olive oil

½ red onion, peeled and diced medium

½ red bell pepper, cored, seeded, and diced medium

1 small or ½ large ripe pineapple, peeled and cut into ½in (1cm) chunks

2 tablespoons good-quality curry powder

1 tablespoon peeled and minced fresh ginger

Pinch allspice

⅓ cup cider vinegar

2 tablespoons dark brown sugar

Kosher salt and freshly cracked black pepper to taste

THE JERK SEASONING

¼ cup cheap yellow mustard

¼ cup red wine vinegar

¼ cup roughly chopped scallions including green tops

3 habanero or Scotch bonnet chile peppers, chopped, including seeds and ribs

3 garlic cloves, peeled

3 tablespoons dried thyme

2 tablespoons dried oregano

2 tablespoons molasses

Spiced pineapple chutney

Light a fire well over to one side of your grill, using enough coals to fill half a shoebox. When the fire has died down and the coals are covered in white ash, then you're ready to cook.

Meanwhile, make the jerk seasoning: Combine the ingredients in a blender or food processor and purée.

Dry the pork with paper towels, season generously with salt and pepper, and rub it all over with the jerk seasoning.

Place the pork roast on the side of the grill away from the coals, being careful that none of the meat is directly over the coals. Put the lid on the grill with the vents open one-quarter of the way and cook, adding a handful of fresh charcoal about every 30 minutes, until the pork is done (5–8 hours). To check for doneness, plunge a big fork straight down into the meat and try to lift it up off the grill—if the fork slides out easily, the meat is done; if the meat hangs on to the fork, give it more time.

While the pork is roasting, make the pineapple chutney: On the stove top, heat the oil in a large sauté pan over medium-high heat until hot but not smoking. Add the onion and bell pepper and sauté, stirring occasionally, until the onion is transparent (7–9 minutes). Stir in the pineapple, curry powder, ginger, and allspice and sauté, stirring occasionally, for about 3 minutes more. Add the vinegar and brown sugar, bring to a boil, lower the heat and simmer gently for 6–8 minutes, stirring occasionally to keep the mixture from sticking to the pan. When the chutney has thickened, remove the pan from the heat, season to taste with salt and pepper, and transfer to a serving dish. (The chutney can be made up to 5 days in advance, covered and refrigerated.)

When the pork is done, remove it from the grill and allow it to cool slightly. When it is cool enough to handle, slice the meat and serve it with the pineapple chutney.

FLAVOR FOOTPRINT WEST INDIES-CARIBBEAN

The flavors of the West Indies reflect the region's complex history. Allspice and Scotch bonnet peppers, for example, originated in the islands, while bananas and coconuts were brought by Europeans, and the widely popular curry powder arrived with Indian indentured servants who were brought in to work the plantations after slavery had ended. From this melting pot of ingredients has come a group of distinctive, boldly flavored cuisines. Just try a couple of the dishes here, and you'll bring the ease and excitement of the islands right into your kitchen.

Red Onion-Tamarind Chutney
Makes about 1½ cups

The unique earthy-tart flavor of tamarind gives this chutney its distinctive taste. We like it with a big, juicy pork roast, although it's also good with beef and lamb.

2 tablespoons olive oil
2 large red onions, peeled and sliced
1 tablespoon peeled and minced fresh ginger
2 tablespoons tamarind paste
1 tablespoon good-quality curry powder
⅓ cup cider vinegar
⅓ cup soft dark brown sugar
Kosher salt and freshly cracked black pepper to taste
3 tablespoons roughly chopped fresh mint

Heat the oil in a large sauté pan over medium-high heat until hot but not smoking. Add the onions and sauté, stirring occasionally, until they are golden brown (11–13 minutes). Add the ginger, tamarind, and curry powder, and sauté, stirring frequently, until fragrant (about 2 minutes more). Add the brown sugar and vinegar and bring to a simmer, stirring to dissolve the sugar. Reduce the heat to low and simmer gently, stirring frequently to prevent scorching, until the chutney thickens (about 10 minutes). Season with salt and pepper, remove from the heat, and stir in the mint. This chutney will keep, covered and refrigerated, for up to 10 days.

West Indian-Style Steak Condiment
Makes about ¾ cup

We may call it "steak condiment"—and it is totally awesome served with a grilled steak—but this is also great with chops.

⅓ cup tamarind pulp
1 tablespoon dry mustard
1 tablespoon minced fresh garlic
1 tablespoon peeled and minced fresh ginger
1 tablespoon minced fresh chile pepper of your choice
1 tablespoon molasses
Kosher salt and freshly cracked black pepper to taste

Place the tamarind pulp in a bowl with enough hot water to cover and let it stand for 30 minutes to soften. Mix the tamarind with all the remaining ingredients and stir well. This condiment will keep, covered and refrigerated, for 3–4 days.

West Indian-Style
Steak Condiment

Guava Barbecue Sauce

Makes about 2 cups

You'll love this one with any kind of meat, fowl, or fish—either brush some on just for the last 30 seconds of grilling time, or pass as an accompaniment, or both.

1 cup ketchup
⅓ cup guava juice (or substitute peach juice)
¼ cup molasses
Juice of 2 limes (about ¼ cup)
2 tablespoons peeled and minced fresh ginger
Kosher salt and freshly cracked black pepper to taste

Combine all the ingredients in a medium bowl and mix well. This sauce will keep, covered and refrigerated, for up to a week.

Pineapple-Curry Relish

Makes about 2 cups

Although we particularly like it with grilled fish or chicken, this is an all-purpose relish that goes with almost anything.

1½ cups small-diced fresh pineapple
Juice of 2 limes (about ¼ cup)
2 tablespoons roughly chopped scallions, green and
  white parts
1 tablespoon minced fresh chile pepper of your choice
1 tablespoon peeled and minced fresh ginger
1 tablespoon curry powder

Combine all the ingredients in a medium bowl and mix well. This relish will keep, covered and refrigerated, for 3–4 days.

SIGNATURE INGREDIENTS/TOP ROW (LEFT TO RIGHT) Tamarind, limes, nutmeg; **SECOND ROW** Ginger, guavas, orange; **THIRD ROW** Coconut, allspice, garlic; **BOTTOM ROW** Curry powder, chiles, oregano.

Adobo Paste

Makes just under 1 cup

This works either as a last-minute rub before chicken, pork, or beef go on the grill, or a quick marinade (up to 4 hours).

¼ cup paprika (not smoked)
3 tablespoons dried oregano
2 tablespoons minced fresh garlic
1 tablespoon ground cumin
1 tablespoon dried red pepper flakes
1 tablespoon minced lime zest
2 tablespoons olive oil
Kosher salt and freshly cracked black pepper to taste

Combine all the ingredients in a small bowl and mix well. This paste will keep, covered and refrigerated, for 2–3 days.

Pineapple-Curry Relish

GRILL-ROASTED, HERB-CRUSTED, BONE-IN PORK LOIN WITH MOSTARDA DI FRUTTA

Pork, fruit, and mustard are one of those trios that just seem right. So we decided to put together an herb-rubbed pork loin with our version of the Italian *mostarda di frutta*, a tasty mix of preserved fruits flavored with mustard seeds. (We use mustard powder and dried fruit to make it easier.) You can use a boneless pork loin in this recipe, but we encourage you to seek out a bone-in one; to us, the meat always seems richer and deeper in flavor.

Serves 6 to 8

THE MEAT

¼ cup olive oil
¼ cup roughly chopped fresh sage
2 tablespoons crushed fennel seed
2 tablespoons minced garlic
1 bone-in, center-cut pork loin, about 5lb (2.25kg)
Kosher salt and freshly cracked black pepper to taste

THE MOSTARDA

1 cup water
½ cup dry mustard
½ cup distilled white vinegar
¼ cup dark brown sugar
1 tablespoon peeled and minced fresh ginger
⅓ cup raisins
⅓ cup each: diced dried apricots, diced dried peaches, diced dried figs, and diced dried mango
Kosher salt and freshly cracked black pepper to taste

Light a fire well over to one side of your grill, using enough coals to fill half a shoebox.

Mash together the oil, sage, fennel, and garlic in a small bowl to form a loose paste. Dry the pork well with paper towels, season it generously with salt and pepper, and rub the pork all over with the seasoning paste.

When the fire has died down and the coals are covered in white ash, place the roast on the side of the grill away from the coals, being careful that none of the meat is directly over the coals. Put the lid on the grill with the vents open one-quarter of the way and cook, adding a handful of fresh charcoal about every 30 minutes, until the pork is done (about 1 hour). To check for doneness, insert a meat thermometer into the center of the roast, without touching the bone; let it sit for 5 seconds, then read the temperature: look for 134°F (57°C) for medium, 150°F (66°C) for medium-well done, and 160°F (71°C) for well done. We like to pull the meat at 147°F (64°C). When the roast is done to your liking, remove it from the grill, cover it loosely with foil, and let it rest for about 20 minutes.

While the pork cooks, make the *mostarda*: Whisk the water and dry mustard together in a small bowl until smooth; set aside. On the stove top, combine the vinegar, sugar, and ginger in a small saucepan over medium-high heat, stirring until the sugar dissolves and the mixture comes to a boil. Reduce the heat to low and simmer, stirring very frequently, until thickened (about 10 minutes). Add the mustard and mix well, then stir in all of the dried fruits and continue to simmer gently until thickened (15–20 minutes more). Add salt and pepper to taste, and transfer to a serving bowl.

To serve, carve the pork between the bone, arrange the meat on a platter, and pass the *mostarda* on the side.

SIMPLE SMOKE-ROASTED WHOLE CHICKENS

This is a classic: Chickens flavored with garlic and rosemary and cooked with the indirect heat and smoke of a slow, low fire. It's the kind of dish you could serve once a week all summer long and not get tired of. And, if you're not familiar with the technique of smoke-roasting (*see also p18*), this is a great dish to start with. It's simple and direct, but ends up with great, smoky flavor.

Serves 6

THE INGREDIENTS

2 whole chickens, 3lb (1.35kg) each
3 tablespoons olive oil
3 tablespoons minced fresh garlic
3 tablespoons roughly chopped fresh rosemary
2 tablespoons kosher salt
2 tablespoons freshly cracked black pepper
2 lemons, halved

Light a fire well over to one side of your grill, using enough coals to fill 1½ large shoeboxes.

Place one chicken on your work surface, breast side up, and push down hard to flatten it as much as possible. Repeat with the second bird, then rub both all over with the olive oil. Mash together the garlic, rosemary, salt, and pepper, and coat the chickens evenly with this herb mixture, pressing gently to be sure it adheres.

When the fire has died down and the coals are covered with white ash, place the chickens on the side of the grill away from the coals, breast side down, legs facing toward the coals, being careful that none of the meat is directly over the coals. Put the lid on the grill with the vents open one-quarter of the way. Cook for 30 minutes, then turn the chickens breast side up, add another ½ shoebox full of fresh charcoal, and continue cooking for 30–45 minutes more. To check for doneness, make a cut into the thickest part of one thigh, all the way to the bone; there should be no sign of pink. (It's not easy to take the temperature of a flattened bird, but if you do use a thermometer, look for a final temperature of 160°F/71°C.)

When the chickens are done, transfer them to a cutting board, cover loosely with foil, and allow them to rest for about 10 minutes. Carve each chicken into 6 pieces, squeeze the lemon halves over them, and serve.

BARBECUE-RUBBED, SMOKE-ROASTED WHOLE CHICKENS WITH APPLE CIDER BARBECUE SAUCE

This is a slightly more complex approach to grilling a whole chicken than the plain-and-simple version on p191, but it's still pretty much a breeze to make. Since the birds are never directly over the coals there's no need to worry about burning sugars, so we can coat them with a simple but luscious ketchup-brown sugar paste before they go onto the grill. We then serve them with a thick, gooey sauce in the traditional barbecue manner.

Serves 6

THE CHICKENS

¾ cup ketchup
2 tablespoons dark brown sugar
1 teaspoon ground coriander
1 teaspoon ground cumin
2 whole chickens, 3lb (1.35kg) each
Kosher salt and freshly cracked black pepper

THE SAUCE

1 cup apple cider
½ cup cider vinegar
2 tablespoons finely minced orange zest
2 tablespoons dark brown sugar
1 tablespoon celery seeds

Light a fire well over to one side of your grill, using enough coals to fill 1½ large shoeboxes.

Combine the ketchup, brown sugar, coriander, and cumin in a small bowl and mix well.

Place one chicken on a work surface, breast side up, and push down hard to flatten it as much as possible. Repeat with the second bird. Sprinkle them generously with salt and pepper and coat thoroughly with the ketchup mixture.

When the fire has died down and the coals are covered with white ash, place the chickens on the side of the grill away from the coals, breast side down, legs facing toward the coals, being careful that none of the meat is directly over the coals. Put the lid on the grill with the vents open one-quarter of the way. Cook for 30 minutes, then turn the chickens breast side up, add another ½ shoebox of fresh charcoal, and continue cooking for 30–45 minutes more. To check for doneness, make a cut into the thickest part of one thigh, all the way to the bone; there should be no sign of pink. (It's not easy to take the temperature of a flattened bird, but if you do use a thermometer, look for a final temperature of 160°F/71°C.)

Meanwhile, make the barbecue sauce on the stove top: Combine the sauce ingredients in a small saucepan over medium-high heat and bring just to a boil. Reduce the heat to low and simmer, stirring frequently, until thick, syrupy, and reduced by about two-thirds (about 20 minutes). Transfer the sauce to a serving bowl.

When the chickens are done, transfer them to a cutting board, cover loosely with foil, and allow them to rest for about 10 minutes. Carve each chicken into 6 pieces and serve, along with the barbecue sauce.

PEPPER-CRUSTED SMOKE-ROASTED TOP LOIN WITH GREEN PEPPERCORN SAUCE

This is a pretty straightforward roast beef with traditional green peppercorn sauce—except, of course, that the beef is coated with a layer of black peppercorns, and roasting it on the grill gives it a lovely deep, smoky flavor that's the perfect complement to the top loin's full-on beefy taste. The decadent sauce makes this a great dish for special occasions.

Serves 10 to 12

THE MEAT

1 beef top loin roast, 6–8lb (2.7–3.6kg)
3 tablespoons olive oil
1 cup freshly cracked black pepper
½ cup kosher salt

THE SAUCE

1 cup brandy
¼ cup green peppercorns, drained and rinsed
2 cups beef stock
1 cup heavy cream
8 tablespoons unsalted butter, diced and kept cold
¼ cup roughly chopped fresh parsley
Kosher salt and freshly cracked black pepper to taste

Light a fire well over to one side of your grill, using enough coals to fill a large shoebox.

Rub the beef with the oil and coat it evenly with the pepper and salt, pressing gently to make sure it adheres.

When the fire has died down and the coals are covered with white ash, place the beef on the side of the grill away from the coals, being careful that none of the meat is directly over the coals. Put the lid on the grill with the vents open one-quarter of the way and cook, adding a handful of fresh charcoal every 30 minutes or so, until the beef is done the way you like it (45 minutes to 1 hour for medium-rare). To check for doneness, poke the roast with your finger to test its firmness (see p37). If you're unsure, insert a meat thermometer in the center of the roast and let it sit for 5 seconds, then read the temperature; you're looking for 120°F (49°C) for rare, 126°F (52°C) for medium-rare, 134°F (57°C) for medium, 150°F (65°C) for medium-well, and 160°F (71°C) for well done. (We like to pull the roast at 122°F/50°C.) When the roast is done, remove it from the grill, cover it loosely with foil, and allow it to rest for at least 15 minutes before carving.

While the beef is cooking, make the sauce on the stove top: Combine the brandy and green peppercorns in a medium sauté pan over medium-high heat. Bring to a boil, adjust the heat to medium, and simmer until the brandy is syrupy (about 3 minutes). Add the beef stock and continue to simmer until reduced by one-third (about 15 minutes more). Stir in the cream and simmer until slightly thickened (about 10 minutes more). Turn the heat to low, then gradually whisk in the cold butter, a few chunks at a time. When all the butter has been added, remove the sauce from the heat and stir in the parsley and salt and pepper.

To serve, cut the beef into slices, arrange them on a platter, and run a ribbon of sauce down the middle of the slices. Pass the remaining sauce on the side.

NORTH CAROLINA-STYLE PULLED PORK BARBECUE WITH TIDEWATER COLESLAW

This is the traditional North Carolina pork barbecue that I (Chris) grew up with. To my mind, there is really no better food than this smoky, fall-apart-tender pork. If you really want to do it right, you should start it at about midnight and stay up all night, drinking beers and telling stories around the fire as the pork cooks. Whenever you cook it, though, it's the perfect meal for large gatherings. It also freezes very well, so don't be afraid of leftovers.

Serves 15

THE MEAT

2 boneless pork butt roasts, 4–5lb
  (1.8–2.25kg) each
3 tablespoons olive oil

THE RUB

4 tablespoons paprika
2 tablespoons kosher salt
2 tablespoons freshly cracked black pepper
2 tablespoons ground cumin
2 tablespoons chile powder
2 tablespoons soft dark brown sugar
1 tablespoon cayenne pepper

THE COLESLAW

1½ cups store-bought mayonnaise
⅓ cup distilled white vinegar
⅓ cup granulated sugar
1 tablespoon celery seeds
1 head green cabbage, finely shredded
2 carrots, finely grated
Kosher salt and freshly cracked black pepper to taste

THE SAUCE

1 cup distilled white vinegar
1 cup cider vinegar
1 tablespoon granulated sugar
1 tablespoon red pepper flakes
1 tablespoon Tabasco
Kosher salt and freshly cracked black pepper to taste

THE EXTRAS

White fluffy sandwich bread or hamburger buns

Light a fire well over to one side of your grill, using enough coals to fill a large shoebox.

Combine the spice rub ingredients in a small bowl and mix well. Rub the pork roasts with the oil and coat them generously with the spice rub, pressing gently to make sure it adheres.

When the fire has died down and the coals are covered with white ash, place the pork on the side of the grill away from the coals, being careful that none of the meat is directly over the coals. Put the lid on the grill with the vents open one-quarter of the way, and cook, adding a handful of fresh charcoal every 30 minutes or so, for 7–9 hours. To test for doneness, stick a big fork in it and try to lift the meat up—if it falls off the fork, it's done.

Meanwhile, make the coleslaw: Combine the mayonnaise, vinegar, sugar, and celery seeds in a large bowl and mix well. Add the cabbage and carrots and toss well to blend. Season with salt and pepper, cover, and refrigerate until serving time.

Now make the barbecue sauce: Combine the vinegars, sugar, pepper flakes, Tabasco, and salt and pepper in a medium bowl and mix well.

Chop or shred the pork (if it's still too hot to handle, use two forks to pull it apart) and mix it with as much of the sauce as you like. Pile it onto the bread or buns, top with the coleslaw, and serve.

SMOKE-ROASTED WHOLE DUCK
WITH ORANGE, GINGER, AND HOISIN-CHILE SAUCE

A whole smoked duck is a beautiful thing to behold—and it's awesomely delicious, too. It's also pretty simple, although you have to remember to start it the day before you want to serve it, since it needs to sit in the refrigerator overnight to absorb the flavors of the sesame, ginger, and orange. The sauce is easy too, but if you're feeling lazy you can just swab the finished duck with a little hoisin sauce.

Serves 2

THE DUCK

1 whole duck, 4–5lb (1.8–2.25kg)
1 tablespoon Asian sesame oil
3 tablespoons freshly cracked white pepper
2 tablespoons peeled and minced fresh ginger
2 tablespoons finely minced orange zest
2 tablespoons kosher salt

THE SAUCE

⅓ cup hoisin sauce
3 tablespoons roughly chopped fresh cilantro
2 tablespoons Asian chile-garlic sauce
1 tablespoon peeled and minced fresh ginger

Use a fork to prick a dozen or so holes through the duck skin in the area between the wing and the breast, making sure you get down to the layer of fat, but being careful not to puncture the meat underneath. Pat the duck dry with paper towels, then rub it all over with the sesame oil.

Combine the white pepper, ginger, orange zest, and salt in a small bowl and mash together; rub this mixture all over the surface of the duck. Put the duck on a plate and refrigerate it overnight, uncovered.

Light a fire well over to one side of your grill, using about enough coals to fill 2 shoeboxes.

Remove the duck from the refrigerator and gently pat it dry again. When the fire has died down and the coals are covered with white ash, put the duck on the side of the grill away from the coals, with the legs closest to the coals. Be careful that none of the duck is directly over the coals. Put the lid on the grill with the vents one-quarter of the way open and cook, adding a ½ shoebox full of fresh charcoal after the first 30 minutes of cooking. About 10 minutes later (after 40 minutes of cooking), reposition the duck so that the breast is closer to the fire. Cook for about another 30–50 minutes. To check for doneness, pierce one of the legs and make sure that the juices run clear; as a second test, twist the leg gently—the joint should feel slightly loose in its socket.

While the duck is roasting, make the sauce: Combine the hoisin, cilantro, chile-garlic sauce, and ginger in a small bowl and mix well.

When the duck is ready, transfer it to a cutting board. To carve, slice straight down to one side of the breastbone, following the shape of the carcass. Repeat on the other side of the breastbone. Cut through the wing joints, and put each duck half on a plate. Top each serving with a drizzle of sauce, and pass the remaining sauce on the side.

CUBAN-STYLE SMOKED PORK SHOULDER WITH CILANTRO VINAIGRETTE

Southerners aren't the only ones who know how to smoke-roast a mean hunk of pork (*see pp196–9*). Cuban cooks are experts in this field, too, so here we add some island flavors to the super-tender, fall-apart smoky meat. We particularly like this served with warm tortillas to wrap around the tendrils of meat.

Serves 8 to 10

THE MEAT

¼ cup minced fresh garlic
¼ cup freshly cracked coriander seeds (or substitute 2 tablespoons ground coriander)
¼ cup paprika
3 tablespoons kosher salt
3 tablespoons freshly cracked black pepper
1 boneless pork shoulder roast, about 6lb (2.7kg)
¼ cup olive oil

THE VINAIGRETTE

⅓ cup extra virgin olive oil
⅓ cup red wine vinegar
¼ cup roughly chopped fresh cilantro
2 tablespoons hot sauce of your choice
1 teaspoon minced fresh garlic
Kosher salt and freshly cracked black pepper to taste

Light a fire well over to one side of your grill, using enough coals to fill a shoebox.

Combine the garlic, coriander, paprika, salt, and pepper in a small bowl and mix well. Rub the pork with the oil and coat it generously with the spice mixture, pressing gently to be sure it adheres.

When the fire has died down and the coals are covered with white ash, place the pork on the side of the grill away from the coals, being careful that none of the meat is directly over the coals. Put the lid on the grill with the vents open one-quarter of the way and cook, adding a handful of fresh charcoal every 30 minutes or so, for 5–8 hours. To test for doneness, stick a big fork in the roast and try to lift it up—if it falls off the fork, it's done.

Meanwhile, make the vinaigrette: Combine the olive oil, vinegar, cilantro, hot sauce, garlic, salt, and pepper in a small bowl and whisk to combine thoroughly.

Chop or shred the pork, drizzle it with the vinaigrette, and serve, either by itself or with hamburger buns or tortillas.

ORANGE AND BOURBON-BRINED BARBECUED WHOLE TURKEY

Here's a Southern-style turkey that's great not just for Thanksgiving, but any time you have a crowd coming over. Brining helps keep the bird moist during the rather rigorous smoking process, so what you end up with is tender meat imbued with a wonderful smoky flavor. (If you want to avoid taking up most of your refrigerator, you can brine the turkey in a large cooler with ice packs floating in it, so long as you change the ice packs frequently.) Good as this is served warm from the grill, it's even better for sandwiches the next day.

Serves 6

THE BRINE

1 gallon (4 liters) water
2 cups kosher salt
1½ cups granulated sugar
1 cup bourbon
2 oranges, sliced

THE TURKEY

12–15lb (5.5–6.5kg) turkey, giblets removed
Freshly cracked black pepper to taste
2 apples (variety of your choice), cored and quartered
1 red onion, peeled and quartered
3 tablespoons roughly chopped fresh sage

Combine the brine ingredients in a large container that the turkey will easily fit into, and stir to dissolve the salt and sugar. Rinse the turkey well inside and out, then place it in the container, making sure it is completely submerged in the brine. Refrigerate for 24–48 hours, turning every 12 hours.

Light a fire well over to one side of your grill, using enough coals to fill a large shoebox. When the fire has died down and the coals are covered with white ash, remove the turkey from the brine and rinse it well, inside and out. Dry the bird with paper towels, sprinkle the cavity generously with pepper, and stuff it with the apples, onion, and sage.

Place the turkey on the side of the grill away from the coals, being careful that none of the bird is directly over the coals. Put the lid on the grill with the vents open one-quarter of the way and cook, adding a handful of fresh charcoal about every 30 minutes, until the juices run clear when you pierce the thigh with a fork (2½–3 hours). Turn the turkey around at least twice during this time, or more often if the side nearest the heat seems to be cooking too quickly. (To double-check doneness with a meat thermometer, insert it in the pit between the breast and leg; when the thermometer reads 160°F/71°C, the bird is done.)

Remove the bird from the grill, cover it loosely with foil, and allow it to rest for at least 15 minutes. Discard the apples and onions and carve it up.

GLAZED SMOKE-ROASTED FRESH HAM
WITH HONEY MUSTARD SAUCE

This is perfect when you're having a group of people over: Delicious, easy to prepare, and unusual enough to cause a bit of comment. If you have the time and inclination to brine it in advance, it will be more tender and flavorful, but it is delicious without brining, too.

Serves 10 to 12

THE MEAT

1 bone-in fresh ham (half an uncured hind leg), 8–10lb (3.5–4.5kg), skin on

1½ cups freshly squeezed orange juice

1½ cups pineapple juice

3 tablespoons roughly chopped fresh sage

25 whole cloves

⅓ cup coarse grainy mustard

⅓ cup honey

THE BRINE (OPTIONAL)

3 quarts (3 liters) water

2 cups dark rum

1 cup dark brown sugar

1 cup kosher salt

2 tablespoons ground allspice

Score diagonal cuts both ways into the skin of the ham with a sharp knife to make a diamond pattern all over it.

If brining the ham, combine the brine ingredients in a container large enough to easily hold the ham and stir to dissolve the salt and sugar. Place the ham in the container, making sure that there is enough liquid to cover it completely. Refrigerate for at least 24 hours and up to 3 days, turning the ham over every 12 hours.

Combine the fruit juices in a small saucepan on the stove top over medium-high heat and bring to a boil. Lower the heat to a simmer and stir frequently, until the mixture is syrupy (about 25 minutes). Stir in the sage and set aside.

Light a fire well over to one side of your grill, using enough coals to fill a large shoebox. Remove the ham from the brine and dry it well with paper towels. (If you did not brine the ham, season it generously with kosher salt and black pepper.) Insert the cloves evenly across the skin in the points of the diamond-shaped cuts.

When the fire has died down and the coals are covered with white ash, place the ham on the side of the grill away from the coals, being careful that none of the meat is directly over the coals. Put the lid on the grill with the vents open one-quarter of the way, and cook, adding a handful of fresh charcoal every 30 minutes or so. Start checking for doneness after 2 hours; it may take up to 3 hours to fully cook. Baste it generously with the fruit juice glaze during the last 30 minutes of cooking. To check for doneness, insert a meat thermometer into the center of the ham and let it sit for 5 seconds, then read the temperature: look for 134°F (57°C) for medium, 150°F (66°C) for medium-well, and 160°F (71°C) for well done; we pull the ham at 147°F (64°C). When the ham is done to your liking, remove it from the grill, cover it loosely with foil, and allow it to rest for 20–30 minutes before carving.

While the ham is resting, combine the mustard and honey in a small bowl and mix well. To serve, carve the ham into thick slices and pass the sauce on the side.

SMOKE-ROASTED OREGANO LEG OF LAMB WITH SWEET AND HOT APRICOTS

Lamb has enough intrinsic flavor to match not only the smokiness that is imparted by a smoldering fire, but also bold spice mixtures, like the lemony oregano paste we use here. And ever since we tasted it on the Greek island of Ikaria, we have loved the combination of lamb and apricots, although this spicy relish is equally delicious with chicken and pork.

Serves 6 to 8

THE MEAT

¼ cup olive oil

¼ cup roughly chopped fresh oregano (or you can use marjoram)

3 tablespoons minced garlic

2 tablespoons finely minced lemon zest

2 tablespoons fennel seed

1 bone-in leg of lamb, 6–8lb (2.7–3.6kg), trimmed of all but ¼in (5mm) surface fat

Kosher salt and freshly cracked black pepper

THE APRICOTS

2 tablespoons olive oil

1 medium red onion, peeled and diced small

1 tablespoon peeled and minced fresh ginger

2 teaspoons red pepper flakes

1 tablespoon ground coriander

1 cup dried apricots, cut into thin strips

½ cup red wine vinegar

2 tablespoons dark brown sugar

Kosher salt and freshly cracked black pepper to taste

Light a fire well over to one side of your grill, using enough coals to fill half a shoebox.

Mash together the oil, oregano, garlic, lemon zest, and fennel seed in a small bowl to make a loose paste. Dry the lamb with paper towels, and sprinkle generously with salt and pepper. With the point of a paring knife, cut 8–10 slits, 2in (5cm) deep, into the meat, and push some of the herb paste into each. Rub any remaining paste over the surface.

When the flames have died down and the coals are covered in white ash, place the lamb on the side of the grill away from the coals, being careful that none of the meat is directly over the coals. Put the lid on with the vents open one-quarter of the way and cook, adding a handful of fresh charcoal about every 30 minutes, until the meat is done how you like it (1½–2 hours for medium-rare). To check for doneness, insert a meat thermometer into the thickest part (without touching the bone), let it sit for 5 seconds, then read it; you're looking for 120°F (49°C) for rare, 126°F (52°C) for medium-rare, 134°F (57°C) for medium, 150°F (65°C) for medium-well, and 160°F (71°C) for well done.

While the lamb is roasting, make the apricots: Heat the oil in a large sauté pan on the stove top over medium-high heat until hot but not smoking. Add the onion and sauté, stirring occasionally, until transparent (7–9 minutes). Add the ginger, red pepper flakes, and coriander and stir until fragrant (about 1 minute). Add the apricots, vinegar, and brown sugar, and bring to a boil. Lower the heat and simmer gently until the apricots are tender (about 5 minutes). Remove from the heat, season with salt and pepper to taste, and transfer to a serving bowl.

When the lamb is done, remove it from the grill, cover loosely with foil, and let it rest for 10–15 minutes. Carve the lamb and serve it with the apricots on the side.

ON A STICK

WE LOVE SKEWERS FOR LOTS OF REASONS:
STRINGING THEM TOGETHER SEEMS LIKE A GAME;
MOST ARE AS EASY TO GRILL AS HOT DOGS; AND
(MAYBE MOST IMPORTANT) YOU CAN GET AWAY
WITH EATING THEM WITH YOUR FINGERS, SO
THEY'RE GREAT PARTY FOOD. AND DID WE
MENTION THEY TASTE WONDERFUL?

THAI CHICKEN STICKS WITH MANGO-CHILE BARBECUE SAUCE

On our last trip to Thailand, we were repeatedly reminded that the ambient level of heat in that cuisine is extreme. These tasty little sticks, fashioned out of chicken tenderloins, are pretty hot for our tastebuds, but would seem relatively mild to even the least chile-loving Thai. The barbecue sauce is also good with grilled fish or pork.

Serves 4 as an appetizer

THE SKEWERS

1lb (450g) chicken tenderloins, tendons removed (12–16 pieces)

2 tablespoons red pepper flakes

1 tablespoon good-quality curry powder

1 tablespoon Asian sesame oil

Kosher salt and freshly cracked black pepper to taste

THE SAUCE

½ cup ketchup

½ cup mango juice

Juice of 2 limes (about ¼ cup)

2 tablespoons Southeast Asian fish sauce (or substitute soy sauce)

1–2 tablespoons Southeast Asian chile-garlic paste, to taste

2 tablespoons peeled and minced fresh ginger

2 tablespoons roughly chopped fresh Thai basil (or substitute Italian basil)

1 tablespoon minced fresh garlic

Build a fire in your grill. When the coals are all ignited, the flames have died down, and the temperature is medium-hot (*see p34*), you're ready to cook.

Combine the barbecue sauce ingredients in a bowl and mix well. Transfer about half the sauce to a small serving bowl and set aside.

Combine the chicken, red pepper flakes, curry powder, oil, and salt and pepper in a bowl, and toss until evenly coated. Thread the tenderloins onto skewers, put them on the grill directly over the coals, and cook until they are just done (3–4 minutes per side). Brush the chicken with the rest of the sauce during the last 30 seconds of cooking. To check for doneness, cut into one to make sure it is opaque all the way through.

Arrange the chicken sticks on a platter with the small serving bowl of sauce for dipping, and serve immediately.

ISTANBUL: KEBAB PARADISE

Sprawling, mysterious, difficult, vigorously young but drenched in faded grandeur, Istanbul is one of the world's premier cities. It's also, as we found when we traveled there, the world capital of kebabs.

Oh, there may be other places in the Middle East or even Southeast Asia where grilled skewers are more pervasive, but in this continent-spanning city they are a class of food unto themselves. Each individual version has a specific history and provenance, so spending time there with our friend Ihsan, who grew up in the city, is a kind of culinary history lesson. One night, arriving after a long drive from Bodrum, in southeastern Turkey, we were startled when Ihsan swerved across traffic to stop at a particular kebab stand. "Cop sis!" he shouted, with his trademark excitement: "Garbage kebabs!" These southeast Anatolian specialties, he explained, used up all the little pieces of whatever was left over in restaurant kitchens at the end of the night— hence the name. And it was like that day after day, as we discovered an incredible profusion of kebab options—simple skewers of tiny livers sprinkled with salt and pepper; chunks of spicy *sucuk* sausage alternating with *kasar* cheese; and infinite variations on the theme of lamb, either ground or in chunks, each with a different name depending on whether it is mixed with, for example, hot pepper paste and the spice mix known as *baharat*, or tomato paste and parsley—and on it went. There is more exotic food on the streets of this fascinating city (fatty, delicious intestine sandwiches, for example), but for sheer variety and inventiveness, the kebabs can't be beat. A plate of these, a glass of the curiously delicious salted yogurt drink called *ayran*, and you'll be happy as a pasha.

GRILLED LAMB SHISH KEBAB
WITH MINTED YOGURT AND SUMAC-SCENTED PITA

This is our tribute to the kefta and shish kebab served at Istanbul's Sultanahmet Keftah restaurant, possibly the best kebab shop in the world. We've added the bell peppers and onions familiar to American backyard cooks. If you can find the spice sumac, its lemony taste adds a distinctly Middle Eastern flavor to the warm pita.

Serves 4

2lb (900g) boneless leg of lamb, cut into
   1in (2.5cm) cubes

2 red onions, peeled and halved, each half quartered

2 red bell peppers, cored, seeded, and halved, each
   half quartered

¼ cup olive oil

Kosher salt and freshly cracked black pepper to taste

Juice of 2 lemons (about ⅓ cup)

¼ cup extra virgin olive oil

¼ cup roughly chopped fresh oregano

1 tablespoon minced garlic

For the yogurt:

1½ cups plain yogurt, whole-milk if possible

½ cup peeled, seeded, and diced cucumber

⅓ cup roughly chopped fresh mint

1 teaspoon ground white pepper

Kosher salt to taste

For the pita:

4 pieces pita bread

2 tablespoons olive oil

1 tablespoon ground sumac (optional)

Build a fire in your grill. When the coals are all ignited, the flames have died down, and the temperature is medium-hot (*see p34*), you're ready to cook.

Combine the yogurt, cucumber, mint, and white pepper in a medium bowl and mix well. Season with salt to taste, cover, and refrigerate.

Combine the lamb, onions, peppers, oil, and salt and pepper in a large bowl and toss to coat. Thread the meat onto skewers, alternating with the peppers and onions. Put the skewers on the grill over the coals and cook until the vegetables are tender and the lamb is done to your liking (4–5 minutes per side for rare). To check for doneness, cut into a cube; the meat should be slightly less done than you like it.

When you put the lamb on the grill, rub the pita with oil and sprinkle with sumac. Place them on the cooler side of the grill and cook until nicely toasted and slightly charred in a few places (2–3 minutes). Remove from the grill and cut each pita into quarters.

When the lamb is done, push the kebabs off the skewers into a bowl, add the lemon juice, oil, oregano, and garlic, and toss gently to coat. Transfer to a platter and serve along with the yogurt and toasted pita.

GRILLED SIRLOIN SKEWERS WITH AROMATIC HERBS, LIME, AND CHILES

In our experience, guests love interactive food—that is, food that they put together themselves. This appetizer, in which the intense flavors of Southeast Asia are combined with the familiar taste of beef, is a perfect example. We like it best set out on a table close to the grill, so guests can gather around and "roll their own" while you cook the main course.

Serves 4 to 6 as an appetizer

THE SKEWERS

1lb (450g) beef sirloin, cut into ½in (1cm) cubes
Kosher salt and freshly cracked black pepper

THE WRAPS

8–12 large lettuce leaves

THE DRESSING

Juice of 1 lime (about 2 tablespoons)
1 tablespoon soy sauce
1 tablespoon Southeast Asian fish sauce (available in Asian markets or large supermarkets)

1 tablespoon peeled and minced fresh ginger
1 tablespoon minced fresh chile peppers of your choice
1 tablespoon roughly chopped fresh mint
1 tablespoon roughly chopped fresh cilantro
1 tablespoon roughly chopped fresh basil

Build a fire in your grill. When the coals are all ignited, the flames have died down, and the temperature is hot (*see p34*), you're ready to cook.

Sprinkle the sirloin cubes generously with salt and pepper, thread them onto skewers, then put them on the grill directly over the coals and cook until they are just done (3–4 minutes per side for medium-rare). To check for doneness, poke the meat with your finger to test its firmness (*see p37*); if you're unsure, cut into one of the cubes to be sure it is slightly less done than you like it.

Push the cooked sirloin off the skewers into a large bowl, add all the dressing ingredients, and toss gently until the meat is evenly and thoroughly coated.

To serve, set out the sirloin cubes and the lettuce leaves on platters and pass them around, so that guests can "roll their own" beef and lettuce rolls.

GRILLED SCALLOP SKEWERS
WITH PINEAPPLE-CURRY RELISH

Scallops are great on the grill: Easy, quick, and with a subtle but distinctive taste. If you make the relish in advance—which is no problem, because it will keep for four or five days in the refrigerator—this is about as fast a dish as you can imagine, yet it has plenty of interest and flavor.

Serves 4 as an appetizer

THE INGREDIENTS

1lb (450g) medium sea scallops (about 16 scallops)
2 tablespoons olive oil
Kosher salt and freshly cracked black pepper
1 recipe Pineapple-Curry Relish (*see p189*)

Build a fire in your grill. When the coals are all ignited, the flames have died down, and the temperature is hot (*see p34*), you're ready to cook.

Rub the scallops with the olive oil and sprinkle them generously with salt and pepper. Thread the scallops onto skewers so that they lie flat, put them on the grill directly over the coals, and cook until they are just opaque throughout (3–4 minutes per side). To check for doneness, poke the scallops with your finger to test their firmness (*see p37*); if you're unsure, cut carefully into one of the scallops to be sure it is just opaque all the way through.

When the scallops are done, transfer the skewers to a platter and serve, passing the relish on the side.

GRILLED CHICKEN AND FIG SKEWERS
WITH PARSLEY-PINE NUT CONDIMENT

With jammy fresh figs and a relish that features rich pine nuts and the gentle astringency of parsley, this dish is a feast of Mediterranean flavors, despite its simplicity. If you can't find fresh figs, you can substitute firm but ripe apricots, halved.

Serves 4

THE INGREDIENTS

2lb (900g) boneless, skinless chicken breasts,
   cut into 1in (2.5cm) cubes
8 fresh ripe figs, halved lengthwise
3 tablespoons olive oil
Kosher salt and freshly cracked black pepper to taste
1 recipe Parsley-Pine Nut Condiment (*see p262*)

Build a fire in your grill. When the coals are all ignited, the flames have died down, and the temperature is medium-hot (*see p34*), you're ready to cook.

Rub the chicken cubes and fig halves with the oil, sprinkle them generously with salt and pepper, and thread them alternately onto skewers so that the fig halves lie flat on their cut sides. Put them on the grill directly over the coals and cook until the figs are nicely browned and the chicken is just done (6–7 minutes per side). To check for doneness, cut into one of the cubes of chicken to be sure it is opaque right through.

When the skewers are done, transfer them to a platter and serve, passing the relish on the side.

GRILLED LEMONGRASS CHICKEN TENDERLOINS WITH CHILE-SOY DIPPING SAUCE

Chicken tenderloins are an excellent option for skewers. Small and (as the name implies) tender, they cook quickly on the grill and provide a good foil for all kinds of strong flavors. The Asian-style dipping sauce we serve with them is delicious with any grilled chicken.

Serves 4 as an appetizer

THE SKEWERS

1lb (450g) chicken tenderloins, tendons removed (12–16 pieces)

3 stalks lemongrass, minced (use the tender, inner portion of the bottom third only)

2 tablespoons Asian sesame oil

Kosher salt and freshly cracked white pepper to taste

THE SAUCE

⅔ cup soy sauce

¼ cup hot chile oil (available at most Asian grocery stores)

3 tablespoons roughly chopped scallions, white and green portions

2 tablespoons peeled and minced fresh ginger

1 teaspoon granulated sugar

Build a fire in your grill. When the coals are all ignited, the flames have died down, and the temperature is medium-hot (*see p34*), you're ready to cook.

Combine the sauce ingredients in a bowl and mix until the sugar dissolves. Transfer to a serving bowl and set aside.

Combine the chicken, lemongrass, sesame oil, and salt and pepper in a bowl and toss until the chicken is evenly coated. Thread the tenderloins onto skewers, place on the grill directly over the coals, and cook until opaque throughout (3–4 minutes per side). To check for doneness, cut into one of the tenderloins to be sure that it is opaque all the way through.

When the tenderloins are done, arrange them on a serving platter along with the dipping sauce and serve right away.

ADOBO PORK SKEWERS

Alive with vibrant flavors, adobo spice paste is a quick way of adding a lot of flavor with little effort. Here we use it to coat strips of pork, which we then thread onto skewers like ribbons and cook quickly over a medium-hot fire. This is a perfect appetizer to serve before a light summer meal.

Serves 4 as an appetizer

THE INGREDIENTS

1lb (450g) boneless pork loin, cut into 16 equal
   strips
1 recipe Adobo Rub (*see p189*)
¼ cup roughly chopped fresh cilantro
2 limes, each cut in half

Build a fire in your grill. When the coals are all ignited, the flames have died down, and the temperature is medium-hot (*see p34*), you're ready to cook.

Rub the pork strips all over with the adobo rub, pressing gently to be sure that it adheres. Thread the pork onto skewers and grill until nicely browned but not charred (5–6 minutes per side for medium). To check for doneness, cut into one of the strips; it should be just slightly less done than you like it.

When the pork is done, transfer the skewers to a serving platter, sprinkle with the cilantro, squeeze over the lime juice, and serve.

SALT AND SZECHUAN PEPPER-GRILLED SHRIMP WITH HOT, SWEET, AND SOUR SPROUT SLAW

What we call Szechuan pepper is actually not a pepper at all; it is the dried berry of a prickly ash tree that grows widely in China. But whatever it may technically be, its tingling heat and unique, citrusy flavor are wonderful. We use it here to enliven grilled shrimp, which we serve with a rather unusual slaw that features mung bean sprouts, an ingredient that has more potential than its often unimaginative use would suggest.

Serves 4 as an appetizer

THE SKEWERS

1lb (450g) medium-large shrimp (16/20 per pound), peeled and deveined

1 tablespoon Asian sesame oil

1 tablespoon kosher salt

1 tablespoon cracked Szechuan peppercorns

THE SLAW

2 cups thinly sliced Napa (Chinese) cabbage

1 cup mung bean sprouts

5 scallions, including green tops, cut lengthwise into thin strips

⅓ cup rice vinegar

3 tablespoons soy sauce

2 tablespoons granulated sugar

2 tablespoons peeled and minced fresh ginger

2 tablespoons roughly chopped fresh mint

2 tablespoons roughly chopped fresh cilantro

2 teaspoons red pepper flakes

Kosher salt and freshly cracked white pepper to taste

Build a fire in your grill. When the coals are all ignited, the flames have died down, and the temperature is medium-hot (*see p34*), you're ready to cook.

Combine the shrimp, sesame oil, salt, and Szechuan pepper in a large bowl, tossing to coat the shrimp evenly. Thread the shrimp onto 4 skewers, arrange them on the grill over the coals, and cook until just done (3–4 minutes per side). To check for doneness, cut into one of the shrimp at its thickest point to be sure it is opaque all the way through.

While the shrimp are cooking, combine the cabbage, bean sprouts, and scallions in a large bowl and toss until well mixed. In another bowl, combine the rice vinegar, soy sauce, sugar, ginger, mint, cilantro, and red pepper flakes, and mix well. Season the dressing to taste with salt and pepper. When the shrimp are done, pour the dressing over the slaw and toss until the cabbage is well coated. Divide the slaw among four salad plates and put a skewer of shrimp on each one.

CURRY-RUBBED GRILLED DUCK SKEWERS WITH PINEAPPLE-GRAPE CHUTNEY

You don't often see duck on skewers, but it is actually very well suited to this treatment. It is no harder to deal with than chicken, but you get a much richer flavor. Be careful not to overcook it, though; unlike chicken, it has the best flavor if served medium-rare or medium. If you don't happen to like the taste of sesame oil, you can simply substitute vegetable oil in this recipe.

Serves 4 to 6 as an appetizer

THE SKEWERS

1lb (450g) boneless duck breast (about 3 single breasts), most of the fat removed, cut into 16 slices

2 tablespoons Asian sesame oil

2 tablespoons good-quality curry powder

1 tablespoon kosher salt

1 tablespoon freshly cracked black pepper

THE CHUTNEY

2 tablespoons olive oil

1 small red onion, peeled and diced small

1 tablespoon peeled and minced fresh ginger

1 tablespoon curry powder

1 cup peeled, cored, and diced fresh pineapple

½ cup seedless red grapes, halved

½ cup cider vinegar

¼ cup packed soft dark brown sugar

Kosher salt and freshly cracked black pepper to taste

Make the chutney: On the stove top, heat the oil in a sauté pan over medium-high heat until hot but not smoking. Add the onions and sauté, stirring occasionally, until transparent (7–9 minutes). Add the ginger and curry powder and continue to sauté, stirring frequently, until fragrant (about 1 minute more). Add the remaining ingredients and bring up to a simmer, stirring to dissolve the sugar. Adjust the heat to low and continue to simmer gently until slightly thickened (5–7 minutes). Remove from the heat, season with salt and pepper, and allow to cool to room temperature before serving. (This chutney will keep, covered and refrigerated, for 4–5 days.)

Build a fire in your grill. When the coals are all ignited, the flames have died down, and the temperature is medium-hot (*see p34*), you're ready to cook.

Rub the duck strips with sesame oil and sprinkle them with the curry powder, salt, and pepper. Thread the duck onto skewers, place on the grill directly over the coals, and cook until nicely browned but not charred (5–7 minutes per side). To check for doneness, cut into one of the duck strips to be sure it is just slightly less done than you like it, to account for carryover cooking. (We like duck breast medium-rare to medium.)

When the duck is done, transfer the skewers to a platter and serve, passing the chutney on the side.

FLAVOR FOOTPRINT CHINA

In many ways, of course, it is ridiculous to talk about a single flavor footprint for a country as huge, with cuisines as varied, as China. But in fact there are a handful of ingredients that, when combined in a dish, evoke the cooking of this country, at least to Western taste buds. Five-spice powder, sesame oil, hoisin sauce, Szechuan peppercorns, and star anise are probably the most distinctive of these, perhaps because they all either originated or were first created in China. With one or two of these easy condiments on hand, you can effortlessly expand your flavor horizon.

All-Purpose Ginger-Soy Barbecue Sauce
Makes about 2 cups

You can use this sauce either as a last-minute finishing glaze or as an accompanying dipping sauce for pretty much anything grilled, from beef to lamb to chicken to vegetables.

½ cup ketchup
½ cup hoisin sauce
½ cup soy sauce
¼ cup rice wine vinegar
3 tablespoons peeled and minced fresh ginger

Combine all the ingredients in a small bowl and mix well. This sauce will keep, covered and refrigerated, for about a week.

Aromatic Rub

Aromatic Rub
Makes just under 1 cup

This fragrant, dry spice rub is wonderful rubbed on chicken or pork before grilling.

¼ cup ground coriander
2 tablespoons ground white pepper
2 tablespoons ground Szechuan peppercorns
2 tablespoons dry mustard
2 tablespoons ground ginger
1 tablespoon kosher salt
1 teaspoon cinnamon

Combine all the ingredients in a small bowl and mix well. Stored in an airtight container and kept in a cool, dark place, this rub will last for a month or longer.

All-Purpose Ginger-Soy Barbecue Sauce

Orange-Ginger Soy Sauce with Cilantro
Makes about 1 cup

We serve this as a sauce partner for just about anything grilled.

½ cup soy sauce
1 tablespoon freshly squeezed orange juice
1 tablespoon grated orange peel
1 tablespoon minced fresh ginger
2 tablespoons rice wine vinegar
2 tablespoons minced fresh cilantro
1 teaspoon granulated sugar
Pinch ground white pepper

Combine all the ingredients in a small bowl and mix well until the sugar dissolves. This sauce will keep, covered and refrigerated, for 2–3 days.

Sesame-Ginger Paste
Makes just under 1 cup

Try rubbing this paste on steak, pork chops, or chicken just before they go on the grill.

⅓ cup peeled and minced fresh ginger
¼ cup Asian sesame oil
2 tablespoons roughly chopped scallions, with green tops
1 tablespoon minced fresh garlic
1 tablespoon minced fresh chile pepper of your choice
1 tablespoon freshly cracked white pepper

Combine all the ingredients in a small bowl and mix well. This paste will keep, covered and refrigerated, for 3–4 days.

SIGNATURE INGREDIENTS/TOP ROW (LEFT TO RIGHT) Five-spice powder, Asian sesame oil, soy sauce; **SECOND ROW** Ginger, chile sauce, rice wine vinegar; **THIRD ROW** Sesame seeds, star anise, white peppercorns; **BOTTOM ROW** Hoisin sauce, garlic, Szechuan pepper.

Sesame-Water Chestnut Relish
Makes about 1 cup

This fragrant, crunchy relish is lovely served alongside grilled fish or chicken.

2 tablespoons sesame seeds
½ cup canned water chestnuts, diced medium
3 tablespoons roughly chopped scallions, with green tops
2 tablespoons Asian sesame oil
1 tablespoon peeled and minced fresh ginger

Toast the sesame seeds on the stove top in a dry skillet over medium heat, shaking them frequently to avoid burning, until they are fragrant and just a shade darker. Combine all the ingredients in a medium bowl and mix well. This will keep, covered and refrigerated, for 2 days.

Sesame-Water Chestnut Relish

GLAZED PORK AND APPLE SKEWERS

Pork and apples make a classic combination; we both first experienced it as children when our grandmothers served us roast pork accompanied by homemade applesauce. Here we put them over the coals, then brush them with a simple but lively glaze enlivened with the licorice-y flavor of caraway. The glaze takes a little while to reduce down, but otherwise, this is a very quick dish to prepare. You could, if you think of it, make the glaze ahead of time, when you're in the kitchen doing something else, anyway. It will keep, covered and refrigerated, for weeks.

Serves 4

THE SKEWERS

2lb (900g) pork tenderloin (2 small tenderloins), cut into 1in (2.5cm) cubes

2 Granny Smith or other green apples, cored, each cut into 8 wedges

3 tablespoons olive oil

Kosher salt and freshly cracked black pepper to taste

THE GLAZE

1½ cups fresh orange juice

½ cup balsamic vinegar

1 tablespoon caraway seeds

1 teaspoon freshly cracked black pepper

Combine the glaze ingredients in a small saucepan and bring to a boil. Reduce the heat to medium and simmer vigorously until the mixture has been reduced by two-thirds and become syrupy (30–40 minutes). Leave to cool.

Meanwhile, build a fire in your grill. When the coals are all ignited, the flames have died down, and the temperature is medium-hot (see p34), you're ready to cook.

Combine the pork, apple wedges, oil, and salt and pepper in a large bowl, and toss gently until evenly coated. Thread the pork and apples alternately onto skewers, put them on the grill directly over the coals, and cook until the apples are golden and slightly softened and the pork is just done (5–6 minutes per side for medium). Brush with the glaze during the last minute of cooking. To check for doneness, poke the pork cubes with your finger to test their firmness (see p37); if you're unsure, cut into one to be sure it is just slightly less done than you like it, to account for carryover cooking.

When the skewers are ready, arrange them on a serving platter, drizzle with some of the remaining glaze, and serve.

GRILLED SWORDFISH SHISH KEBAB
WITH MANGO-GINGER RELISH

Although in Turkey, where the term comes from, "shish kebab" means anything grilled on a skewer, in the US it has come to denote the particular arrangement of cubes of meat alternating on a skewer with bell peppers and onions. Here we substitute swordfish steak for the beef, which gives the kebab a more delicate flavor. Fortunately, this fish has a firm enough texture to stand up to the treatment.

Serves 4

THE INGREDIENTS

2lb (900g) swordfish steak, about 1in (2.5cm) thick, cut into 1in (2.5cm) cubes

2 red bell peppers, cored, seeded, and halved, each half quartered

1 red onion, peeled and halved, each half quartered

¼ cup olive oil

Kosher salt and freshly cracked black pepper to taste

1 recipe Mango-Ginger Relish (*see p115*)

Build a fire in your grill. When the coals are all ignited, the flames have died down, and the temperature is medium-hot (*see p34*), you're ready to cook.

Combine the swordfish, red peppers, onion, oil, and salt and pepper in a large bowl and toss until evenly coated. Thread the fish, red peppers, and onion alternately onto skewers, put them on the grill directly over the coals, and cook until the vegetables are tender and the swordfish is just done (4–5 minutes per side). To check for doneness, poke the fish with your finger to test its firmness (*see p37*); if you're unsure, cut into one of the cubes; it should be just opaque throughout.

When the skewers are done, transfer them to a serving platter and serve, passing the relish on the side.

LAMB AND PEACH SKEWERS
WITH CUCUMBER-FETA RELISH

Although the flavors of this dish are most closely identified with Greece, it seems a little Persian as well, with the lushly aromatic peaches and the meaty, slightly sweet lamb. If you're lucky enough to have any leftovers, you can make a very delicious sandwich by piling everything into a pita pocket.

Serves 4

THE SKEWERS

2lb (900g) boneless leg of lamb, cut into 1in (2.5cm) cubes

2 ripe but firm peaches, pitted and cut into eighths

2 red bell peppers, cored, seeded, and halved, each half quartered

1 red onion, peeled and halved, each half quartered

¼ cup olive oil

1 tablespoon minced garlic

1 tablespoon dried oregano

Kosher salt and freshly cracked black pepper to taste

THE RELISH

1 cucumber, peeled and diced small

8oz (225g) feta cheese, diced medium

¼ cup roughly chopped fresh mint

¼ cup extra virgin olive oil

2 tablespoons red wine vinegar

Kosher salt and freshly cracked black pepper to taste

Build a fire in your grill. When the coals are all ignited, the flames have died down, and the temperature is medium-hot (see p34), you're ready to cook.

Combine the lamb, peaches, red peppers, onion, oil, garlic, oregano, and salt and pepper in a large bowl and toss gently. Thread the lamb, peach, red pepper, and onion alternately onto skewers, place on the grill directly over the coals, and cook until the vegetables are tender and the meat is just done (4–5 minutes per side for rare). To check for doneness, poke the lamb with your finger to test its firmness (see p37); if you're unsure, cut into one of the cubes and check that it is slightly less done than you like it, to account for carryover cooking.

While the skewers cook, combine the relish ingredients in a medium-sized bowl and toss gently to combine.

When the skewers are ready, transfer them to a platter and serve, passing the relish on the side.

SALADS FROM THE GRILL

OPEN-FACED GRILLED SIRLOIN AND TOMATO SANDWICHES

Okay, so maybe this isn't precisely a sandwich. In fact, it's sort of a grilled steak kebab salad, featuring lightly grilled cherry tomatoes, that you pile on top of thick slices of grilled bread. But when you get a bite of that rich, meaty sirloin along with the fresh-tasting vinaigrette and the crusty bread with the tomato juices soaked into it, you're really not going to care what it's called. It's just plain delicious.

Serves 4

THE SALAD

2lb (900g) beef sirloin tips, cut into 1½in (3.5cm) cubes

2 tablespoons vegetable oil

2 tablespoons freshly cracked cumin seeds (or substitute 1 tablespoon ground cumin)

Kosher salt and freshly cracked black pepper to taste

16 cherry tomatoes

4 slices of good French bread, about 1in (2.5cm) thick

THE DRESSING

½ small red onion, peeled and diced small

½ cup roughly chopped fresh parsley

⅓ cup extra virgin olive oil

¼ cup balsamic vinegar

1 tablespoon minced fresh garlic

3–6 dashes Tabasco sauce, or to taste

Kosher salt and freshly cracked black pepper to taste

Build a fire in your grill. When the coals are all ignited, the flames have died down, and the temperature is medium-hot (see p34), you're ready to cook.

Combine the vinaigrette ingredients in a large bowl, mix well, and set aside.

Combine the sirloin tips, oil, cumin, and salt and pepper in a large bowl and toss until the tips are evenly coated. Thread the tips onto skewers, put them on the grill directly over the coals, and cook until they are just done (5–7 minutes per side for medium-rare). To check for doneness, poke the meat with your finger to test its firmness (see p37); if you're unsure, cut into one of the tips; it should be slightly less done than you like it.

While the meat is cooking, thread the cherry tomatoes onto skewers, put them on the grill next to the meat, and cook just until the tomatoes are lightly colored but not cooked through (about 2 minutes per side). Arrange the bread slices around the perimeter of the fire and cook until lightly toasted (about 2 minutes per side).

When the meat and the tomatoes are done, gently push them off their skewers into the bowl containing the vinaigrette, then toss gently to coat.

To serve, place a slice of toast on each plate, spoon the sirloin and tomatoes evenly over the toasts, and serve immediately.

WATERCRESS, GRILLED SHRIMP, AND MANGO SALAD WITH SESAME-SOY DRESSING

The combination of peppery greens, lush grilled shrimp, and sweet fruit gives you a very flavorful, interesting salad that is both substantial and refreshing. Here we serve it with a slightly piquant dressing that combines a range of wonderful Asian flavors. You can leave out the fish sauce if you like, but the dressing will not have as deep a flavor.

Serves 4 as a salad course or appetizer

THE SALAD

1lb (450g) extra large (12 or less per pound) shrimp, peeled and deveined

2 tablespoons vegetable oil

1 tablespoon five-spice powder

Kosher salt and freshly cracked black pepper to taste

2 bunches watercress, trimmed, washed, and dried

2 ripe but firm mangoes, peeled, pitted, and cut into chunks

THE DRESSING

¼ cup extra virgin olive oil

¼ cup Asian sesame oil

¼ cup soy sauce

2 tablespoons distilled white vinegar

2 tablespoons peeled and minced fresh ginger

1 teaspoon granulated sugar

4 dashes Tabasco sauce

2 tablespoons Southeast Asian fish sauce (available in Asian markets or large supermarkets)

Build a fire in your grill. When the coals are all ignited, the flames have died down, and the temperature is medium-hot (*see p34*), you're ready to cook.

Combine all the dressing ingredients in a small bowl, whisk to blend well, then set aside.

Rub the shrimp with oil, sprinkle with five-spice powder, salt, and pepper, and thread onto skewers. Put them over the coals and grill until they are opaque all the way through (3–4 minutes per side), then remove from the grill and allow to cool to room temperature (about 15 minutes).

Put the watercress in a large bowl, slide the grilled shrimp off the skewers onto the watercress, then add the mangoes. Whisk the dressing again to blend, add just enough to moisten the salad (there will probably be some dressing left over), toss well, and serve.

SPINACH AND GRILLED PEACH SALAD
WITH BLUE CHEESE, BACON, AND SWEET-AND-SOUR DRESSING

If you've never had grilled fruit before, peaches are a perfect introduction; just a few minutes over the coals adds a trace of smoky char that is the perfect complement to their natural sweetness. Put them together with fresh spinach and a crumble of blue cheese and bacon, and you've got a salad (*see overleaf*) that is fantastic on its own but also makes a great appetizer before a simple steak dinner.

Serves 4 as a salad course or appetizer

THE SALAD

8 strips bacon

2 ripe but firm peaches, halved and pitted

2 tablespoons olive oil

2 bunches baby spinach leaves, trimmed, washed, and dried

½ cup crumbled blue cheese of your choice

THE DRESSING

2 tablespoons ketchup

2 tablespoons grainy mustard

1 tablespoon granulated sugar

1 teaspoon minced fresh garlic

¾ cup extra virgin olive oil

¼ cup balsamic vinegar

Juice of I lime (about 2 tablespoons)

Kosher salt and freshly cracked black pepper to taste

Build a fire in your grill. When the coals are all ignited, the flames have died down, and the temperature is medium-hot (*see p34*), you're ready to cook.

On the stove top, cook the bacon in a sauté pan over medium heat until crisp (6–8 minutes). Drain off any fat and let the bacon cool until you are able to handle it, then crumble it roughly between your fingers into a small bowl.

Make the dressing: Combine the ketchup, mustard, sugar, and garlic in a blender or food processor and purée. With the machine running, add the oil in a slow, steady stream. When all the oil is incorporated, add the vinegar and lime juice and pulse to combine. Season with salt and pepper to taste.

Rub the peach halves with oil, sprinkle them with salt and pepper, then put over the coals and grill, cut sides down, until nicely browned (4–5 minutes). Remove from the grill, cut each half into 4 wedges, and transfer to a large bowl, along with the spinach.

Pulse the dressing a few more times to blend; add enough dressing to the peaches and spinach just to moisten (there will probably be some dressing left over), and toss to coat. Arrange the salad on a platter or individual serving plates, sprinkle generously with the blue cheese and bacon, and serve.

SMOKY EGGPLANT AND GRILLED PEPPER SALAD WITH BRAISED GARLIC, POMEGRANATE MOLASSES, AND MINT

If you look at American cuisine, you might think that the idea of grilling vegetables was invented in the 1980s. But in the Middle East there is an ancient and enduring relationship between vegetables and live fire. This substantial salad is in the mezze tradition of that part of the world, and uses some of its classic flavors. If you already have a fire going, you can ash-roast the garlic in advance, wrapped in a double layer of foil (*see* Hobo Packs, *p302*); otherwise, braise it gently in the oven for that authentic taste and texture.

Serves 4 as a salad course or appetizer

THE SALAD

2 medium eggplants, sliced into rounds about ½ in (1cm) thick
2 red bell peppers, cored, seeded, and halved
¼ cup olive oil
Kosher salt and freshly cracked black pepper to taste
2 pieces pita bread
2 tablespoons extra virgin olive oil
1 tablespoon freshly cracked coriander seeds (or substitute 1½ teaspoons ground coriander)

THE DRESSING

1 head of garlic
Juice of 1 lemon (about ¼ cup)
⅓ cup extra virgin olive oil
¼ cup roughly chopped fresh mint
2 tablespoons pomegranate molasses
1 teaspoon ground cumin
Kosher salt and freshly cracked black pepper to taste

Braise the garlic for the dressing: Heat the oven to 300°F (150°C); slice the top quarter off the head, set it on a sheet of foil and sprinkle with a little oil, salt, and pepper, then wrap and braise until soft (about 1 hour).

Build a multilevel fire in your grill (*see p31*). When the coals are all ignited, the flames have died down, and the temperature is medium-hot (*see p34*), you're ready to cook.

In a large bowl, combine the eggplant, pepper, oil, and salt and pepper and toss gently. Put the vegetables on the hotter side of the grill and cook, turning once, until slightly browned (4–5 minutes per side for the eggplant; 3–4 per side for the peppers). Put them back into the bowl you originally tossed them in.

While the vegetables cook, rub the pitas with oil, sprinkle with coriander, and place on the side of the grill with fewer coals. Cook until nicely toasted and slightly charred here and there (2–3 minutes). Cut them into wedges.

Make the dressing: Making sure the garlic is cool enough to handle, squeeze the flesh from each clove and mash with the lemon juice in a small bowl. Add the remaining ingredients and mix well. Pour the dressing over the vegetables and toss gently. Transfer the salad to a serving dish and serve, accompanied by the grilled pita bread.

ROMAINE AND AVOCADO SALAD
WITH GRILLED CHILE SHRIMP AND LIME-CUMIN DRESSING

This salad is our tribute to Caesar Cardini, the Mexican restaurateur who is credited with inventing in 1924 what today is the single most popular salad in the United States—the Caesar. While this one is quite different, its crunchy texture and the Mexican flavors of lime, cilantro, cumin, chile, and avocado make it equally appealing.

Serves 4 as a salad course or appetizer

THE SALAD

1lb (450g) medium-large (16/20 per pound) shrimp, peeled and deveined

2 tablespoons olive oil

1 teaspoon chile powder

Kosher salt and freshly cracked black pepper to taste

1 large head romaine lettuce, washed, dried, and cut crosswise into 2in (5cm) pieces

12 cherry tomatoes, washed, dried, and stemmed

2 ripe but firm avocados, halved, pitted, peeled, and each half cut into 3 wedges

THE DRESSING

Juice of 3 limes (about ⅓ cup)

⅓ cup extra virgin olive oil

2 tablespoons roughly chopped fresh cilantro

1 teaspoon minced garlic

1 teaspoon ground cumin

Kosher salt and freshly cracked black pepper to taste

Build a fire in your grill. When the coals are all ignited, the flames have died down, and the temperature is medium-hot (*see p34*), you're ready to cook.

In a large bowl, whisk the dressing ingredients together well.

In another bowl, combine the shrimp, oil, chile powder, and salt and pepper and mix well to coat the shrimp evenly. If desired, thread the shrimp onto skewers; otherwise, arrange them on the hot side of the grill. Cook until just done (3–4 minutes per side). To check for doneness, carefully cut into one of the shrimp at its thickest point and peek inside to be sure it is just opaque all the way through.

While the shrimp are cooking, divide the lettuce, cherry tomatoes, and avocado wedges among four salad plates.

Transfer the cooked shrimp to the bowl of dressing (pushing them off the skewers, if you used them) and mix gently. Arrange the shrimp on each salad, spoon the remaining dressing over the top, and serve.

SPAIN: DISCOVERING SMALL BITES

We first came across tapas nearly 30 years ago in the tiny, somewhat decrepit working-class bars of Madrid. We walked into the first of these minuscule joints—nothing more than a long, narrow bar with a few stools and some standing room—at random, in search of a mid-afternoon beer.

At first we were puzzled by the fact that the floor was literally covered, like a carpet of fallen leaves, with scraps of paper. Then we discovered the primary pastime of the patrons—gambling. For a couple of pesetas, you bought little slips of paper and tore them open to see if you had won anything. Imitating the regulars at the bar, we bought them by the handful and sat there opening them and throwing them away like so many peanut shells. And, like everyone else, we accompanied our triumphs and disappointments with many little glasses of beer or Rioja and an endless succession of the savory snacks known as tapas that were lined up on the bar, each impaled with a toothpick. Oddly, each time we ate one and discarded the toothpick, we noticed that the bartender would carefully place a clean toothpick on a plate in front of us. After many quizzical looks and shrugs of the shoulders, we finally figured out that he calculated the bill according to the pile of toothpicks in front of you, each tapa costing exactly the same. A chunk of spicy chorizo, a trio of smoky arbequina olives, a fresh fig topped with a smidgen of Cabrales cheese, a single slice of acorn-fed ham—each was a tiny treat of intense, deep flavor. Today tapas are globally known and immensely popular. Wherever I find them, though, they always take me back to those lazy, innocent afternoons of what we like to think of as true cultural exploration.

GRILLED FIGS
WITH BLUE CHEESE AND CRISPY HAM

We love the rich flavor and jammy texture of grilled figs, here perfectly matched with tangy blue cheese and lightly crisped ham. For the most Spanish-tasting dish, use Serrano ham and Cabrales cheese. If they're not available, though, you can use prosciutto and any good-quality blue cheese. Our friends Valerie and Ihsan Gurdal, of Formaggio Kitchen in Boston and New York, insist that you should use whatever variety of blue cheese is made closest to you; we're sure that, as usual, they're right.

Serves 4 as an appetizer

8 fresh ripe figs, halved lengthwise
2 tablespoons olive oil
Kosher salt and freshly cracked black pepper to taste
8 slices Serrano ham (or substitute prosciutto), halved lengthwise into strips
4oz (115g) Cabrales or other blue cheese of your choice, crumbled

Build a fire in your grill. When the coals are all ignited, the flames have died down, and the temperature is medium (*see p34*), you're ready to cook.

Toss the figs with the olive oil in a medium bowl and sprinkle with salt and pepper. Place on the grill directly over the coals, cut side down, and cook until just nicely browned (3–4 minutes).

Put the ham on the grill directly over the coals and cook just until crispy (about 1 minute).

Top each fig with some of the cheese and the crisp ham. Serve warm or at room temperature.

SOUTHEAST ASIAN-STYLE NAPA CABBAGE SALAD WITH CHILE-CRUSTED GRILLED CHICKEN AND PEANUT-LIME DRESSING

Cooks in the tropical world have a tendency to turn to cabbage for their salads, since it holds up better in hot weather than more tender greens. We like it because it has a nice little bite to it, and also has a great crunchy consistency. Here it provides the perfect foil for a lively peanut-lime dressing and grilled chicken breasts given mouth-searing tropical heat with a rub of chiles and white pepper.

Serves 4 as an entrée

THE SALAD

2–4 tablespoons minced fresh chile peppers of your choice, to taste

2 tablespoons freshly cracked white pepper (or substitute black pepper)

3 tablespoons kosher salt

4 boneless, skinless split chicken breasts (cutlets), about 8oz (225g) each

½ head Napa cabbage, cut crosswise into thin strips

1 red bell pepper, halved, seeded, and cut into thin strips

½ cup loosely packed fresh basil leaves

½ cup loosely packed fresh cilantro leaves

⅓ cup loosely packed fresh mint leaves

THE DRESSING

Juice of 2 limes (about ¼ cup)

3 tablespoons Southeast Asian fish sauce (available in Asian markets or large supermarkets)

2 tablespoons finely chopped unsalted roasted peanuts

1 tablespoon granulated sugar

1 tablespoon peeled and minced fresh ginger

1 teaspoon minced fresh garlic

Build a fire in your grill. When the coals are all ignited, the flames have died down, and the temperature is medium-hot (*see p34*), you're ready to cook.

Combine all the dressing ingredients in a small bowl, whisk to blend well, then set aside.

Combine the minced chiles, white pepper, and salt in another small bowl and mix well. Rub the chicken generously with this spice mixture, then put it over the coals and grill until opaque all the way through (6–8 minutes per side, depending on thickness). To check for doneness, cut into one cutlet and peek in to be sure that it is opaque all the way through. Set the chicken aside to cool slightly.

Combine the cabbage, bell pepper, and herbs in a large bowl. Slice the chicken crosswise into thin strips, then cut the slices into bite-size pieces and add to the salad. Stir the dressing again, add just enough to moisten the salad (there will probably be some dressing left over), toss to coat, and serve.

LATIN-STYLE CABBAGE SALAD
WITH GRILLED PORK AND PINEAPPLE

This entrée salad is inspired by our favorite version of the classic Costa Rican lunch known as *casado*, which consists of a cabbage salad, a piece of pork, and some rice and beans. Here we've put the pork right into the salad and added pineapple for sweetness and texture. We admit that we've cheated a bit by adding the chipotle, which is really Mexican, but we think its smoky heat is the perfect complement to the grilled fruit and meat.

Serves 4

THE SALAD

1 pork tenderloin, about 12–14oz (350–400g), trimmed and cut into ½in (2cm) cubes

1 small or ½ large ripe pineapple, peeled and cut into ½in (2cm) cubes (about 1 cup)

2 tablespoons olive oil

Kosher salt and freshly cracked black pepper to taste

3 tablespoons cumin seeds

1 small head green cabbage, cored and diced large

1 red bell pepper, seeded and diced medium

1 carrot, peeled and diced medium

½ cup loosely packed fresh cilantro leaves

THE DRESSING

1 cup pineapple juice or orange juice

¾ cup extra virgin olive oil

Juice of 2 limes (about ¼ cup)

3 tablespoons minced canned or jarred chipotle peppers in adobo sauce

1 tablespoon minced fresh garlic

Kosher salt and freshly cracked black pepper to taste

Make the dressing: On the stove top, bring the fruit juice to a boil in a small pan over high heat, then lower the heat and simmer until reduced to a syrupy consistency (25–30 minutes). Remove from the heat and allow to cool to room temperature. Add the olive oil, lime juice, chipotles, garlic, and salt and pepper, mix well, and set aside.

Build a fire in your grill. When the coals are all ignited, the flames have died down, and the temperature is medium (*see p34*), you're ready to cook.

Combine the pork and pineapple cubes in a large bowl, add the oil and salt and pepper, and toss to coat. Thread the cubes alternately onto skewers, then put over the coals and grill until the pork is well seared and done to your liking (5–6 minutes per side for medium). To check for doneness, cut into one of the pork cubes; the meat should be just slightly less done than you like it. Set the skewers aside to cool slightly.

Toast the cumin seeds in a dry skillet over the fire (or on the stove top over medium heat), shaking them frequently to prevent burning, until they become fragrant and just a shade darker (3–5 minutes).

Combine the cabbage, red pepper, carrot, and cilantro in a large bowl. Push the pork and pineapple off the skewers into the bowl. Stir the dressing again, add just enough to moisten the salad ingredients (there will probably be some left over), and toss to coat. Sprinkle the toasted cumin seeds over the salad and serve.

GRILLED CURRY CHICKEN WITH WATERCRESS, GRAPES, PEACHES, AND ORANGE-RED WINE VINAIGRETTE

As you cook the curry-coated chicken in this dish, the marvelous aroma that rises up from the grill will give you a clear idea of how the heat brings out the flavor of spices. It's important to use a good curry powder here, since the lesser ones can have a chalky quality. To balance the spiciness of the curry, we add sweet grapes and peaches along with pleasantly bitter watercress for an exciting flavor trifecta.

Serves 4 as a salad course or appetizer

THE SALAD

2 boneless, skinless split chicken breasts (cutlets), about 8oz (225g) each
2 tablespoons olive oil
1 tablespoon good-quality curry powder
Kosher salt and freshly cracked black pepper
2 bunches watercress, trimmed, washed, and dried well
20 green grapes, stemmed, halved, and deseeded
2 ripe but firm peaches, pitted and sliced into 8 sections

THE DRESSING

1 cup fresh orange juice
⅓ cup extra virgin olive oil
⅓ cup red wine vinegar
2 tablespoons roughly chopped fresh parsley
Kosher salt and freshly cracked black pepper to taste

Make the dressing: On the stove top, bring the orange juice to a boil in a small pan over high heat, then lower the heat slightly and simmer until reduced in volume to ¼ cup (about 20 minutes). Remove from the heat and allow to cool to room temperature. Add the oil, wine vinegar, parsley, salt, and pepper, whisk together, and set aside.

Build a fire in your grill. When the coals are all ignited, the flames have died down, and the temperature is medium (*see p34*), you're ready to cook.

Coat the chicken breasts with oil, rub them all over with the curry powder, and sprinkle them generously with salt and pepper. Place them on the grill directly over the coals and cook until they are browned on the outside and just cooked through (6–8 minutes per side). To check for doneness, poke the chicken with your finger to test its firmness (*see p37*); if you're unsure, make a cut in the thickest part of one of the breasts and check to be sure that it is opaque all the way through. When the breasts are done, transfer them to a plate and cover them loosely with foil to keep warm.

While the chicken is cooking, combine the watercress, grapes, and peaches in a large bowl. Stir the dressing again, add to the watercress-fruit mixture, and toss well to coat. Divide the salad among four plates.

Slice the chicken on the bias into strips, arrange the strips on top of each salad, and serve.

GRILLED ARTICHOKE, ARUGULA, AND RADICCHIO SALAD WITH LEMON-FETA DRESSING

To us, artichokes have a rather meaty flavor, which makes them a natural for the grill. The slight bitterness of the arugula and radicchio in this salad provides a good complement to the mellowness of the artichoke, and the Greek flavors of the dressing bring it all together.

Serves 4 as a salad course or appetizer

THE SALAD

4 artichokes
1 red bell pepper, cored, seeded, and halved
1 small red onion, peeled and sliced in ½ in (1cm) thick rounds (keep rings together)
¼ cup olive oil
Kosher salt and freshly cracked black pepper
1 bunch arugula, trimmed, washed, and dried well
1 head radicchio, cored and sliced into thin strips

THE DRESSING

½ cup crumbled feta cheese
⅓ cup extra virgin olive oil
Juice of 1 lemon (about ¼ cup)
2 tablespoons roughly chopped fresh parsley
1 teaspoon minced garlic
Kosher salt and freshly cracked black pepper to taste

On the stove top, bring a large pot of salted water to a boil over high heat. While the water is heating, trim the artichoke stems, snap off the coarse outer leaves, then cut 1in (2.5cm) off the top of each artichoke. Quarter each artichoke and remove the hairy-looking "choke" from each quarter. Add the artichoke quarters to the boiling water, adjust the heat to low, and simmer until tender (15–20 minutes). Drain, cool in a bowl of ice water, and drain well again. Set aside.

Build a fire in your grill. When the coals are all ignited, the flames have died down, and the temperature is hot (*see p34*), you're ready to cook.

Rub the poached artichoke hearts, bell peppers, and onion slices with oil and sprinkle generously with salt and pepper. Put the vegetables on the grill and cook until golden brown and slightly charred (5–7 minutes per side). Transfer the grilled artichoke hearts and onions to a large bowl, separating the onions into rings; cut the grilled peppers into strips and add them to the bowl, along with the arugula and radicchio.

Whisk together all the dressing ingredients in a medium bowl (the dressing will be chunky). Add the dressing to the salad gradually, tossing very gently as you go along until everything is lightly and evenly coated.

PEPPER-CRUSTED GRILLED FLANK STEAK SALAD WITH TOMATOES AND BASIL

On those hot summer days when you want a meal that is light but still satisfying, this Mediterranean-inspired salad is the perfect solution. It's particularly good in late summer when tomatoes are at their peak and basil is most flavorful. Be sure to cut the flank steak very thin and on the bias, so it is nice and tender.

Serves 4 as an entrée

THE SALAD

¼ cup freshly cracked black pepper
3 tablespoons kosher salt
1lb (450g) flank steak or top round
1 bunch arugula, trimmed, washed, and dried
1 cup loosely packed small fresh basil leaves
4 vine-ripened tomatoes (preferably beefsteak), about the size of baseballs, cored and sliced about 1in (2.5cm) thick

THE DRESSING

⅓ cup top-quality extra virgin olive oil
3 tablespoons top-quality balsamic vinegar
Kosher salt and freshly cracked black pepper to taste

Build a fire in your grill. When the coals are all ignited, the flames have died down, and the temperature is hot (*see p34*), you're ready to cook.

Combine the ¼ cup black pepper and 3 tablespoons salt in a small bowl and mix well. Rub the steak generously with this mixture, lay it over the coals, and grill until almost done to your taste (5–7 minutes per side, depending on thickness, for medium-rare). To check for doneness, poke the steak with your finger to test its firmness (*see p37*); if you're unsure, make a cut in the thickest part and peek inside to be sure that it is slightly less done than you like it. Set the steak aside to cool slightly.

Scatter the arugula and basil leaves over a large platter to cover. Lay the tomato slices on top. Slice the steak crosswise as thinly as possible, then cut the slices in half and arrange them over the tomatoes. Drizzle the oil over the salad, followed by the balsamic vinegar, then sprinkle generously with salt and pepper and serve immediately.

FLAVOR FOOTPRINT
EASTERN MEDITERRANEAN-NORTH AFRICA

There are important distinctions among the many cuisines of the eastern Mediterranean and North Africa. However, they do all share a basic approach to flavor, as well as many common ingredients. Nuts are very prevalent in these cuisines, as are honey, a wide range of highly aromatic, often floral spices, and many types of ground dried chiles, from relatively mild to quite hot. We think these cuisines are poised to skyrocket in popularity, and this handful of make-ahead flavoring dishes lets you bring their exotic allure to your own table.

North African Chile Paste
Makes about ¾ cup

This all-purpose chile condiment will accompany almost anything perfectly—or use it as a wet rub for chicken or pork just before you grill them.

¼ cup dried red chiles, finely crushed
2 tablespoons coriander seeds, crushed
2 tablespoons minced garlic
1 tablespoon cumin seeds
1 tablespoon caraway seeds
1 tablespoon kosher salt
1 tablespoon freshly cracked black pepper
5 tablespoons vegetable oil

Combine all the ingredients in a small bowl, or, if you prefer a finer paste, mash in a mortar and pestle. This paste will keep, covered and refrigerated, for 2–3 days.

Parsley-Pine Nut Condiment
Makes about 1 cup

Great served as an accompaniment for lamb, chicken, or fish, or sprinkled on grilled vegetables.

⅓ cup pine nuts
⅓ cup roughly chopped fresh parsley
¼ cup extra virgin olive oil
1 tablespoon finely minced lemon zest
1 teaspoon minced fresh garlic
Kosher salt and freshly cracked black pepper to taste

Toast the pine nuts in a shallow baking pan in a 350°F (180°C) oven until they are golden (5–10 minutes), or in a dry skillet over medium heat for 2–3 minutes, shaking frequently to avoid burning. Combine all the ingredients in a small bowl and mix well. This condiment is best used the day it is made, but it will keep, covered and refrigerated, for 3 days.

North African
Chile Paste

Peach Relish with Cumin and Mint
Makes about 2 cups

Try this as an accompaniment to grilled chicken, fish, or pork.

2 large, ripe but firm peaches, pitted and diced small
¼ cup roughly chopped fresh mint
Juice of 1 lemon (about ¼ cup)
2 tablespoons cumin seeds
Kosher salt and freshly cracked black pepper to taste

Combine all the ingredients in a medium bowl and mix well. This relish will keep, covered and refrigerated, for 3–4 days.

Dill-Pomegranate Butter
Makes about ½ cup

Put a dab or chilled slice of this on chicken or fish when it comes off the grill.

½ cup unsalted butter, softened
2 tablespoons pomegranate seeds
1 tablespoon roughly chopped fresh dill
Kosher salt and freshly cracked black pepper to taste

Combine all the ingredients in a small bowl and mash together until evenly blended. This butter will keep, wrapped in wax paper and refrigerated, for about 1 week. (Because of the fresh pomegranate seeds, it does not freeze well.)

SIGNATURE INGREDIENTS/TOP ROW (LEFT TO RIGHT)
Cardamom, walnuts, dried chiles, dill; **SECOND ROW** Saffron, sumac, cinnamon, pistachio nuts; **THIRD ROW** Dried limes, oregano, pine nuts, pomegranate molasses; **BOTTOM ROW** Parsley, fenugreek, rosewater, mint.

Exotic Mediterranean Rub
Makes about 1 cup

This dry spice mix works best rubbed on lamb or chicken that's ready to grill.

¼ cup sesame seeds
⅓ cup coriander seeds, crushed
2 tablespoons ground fenugreek
2 tablespoons dried oregano
1 tablespoon ground cumin
1 tablespoon kosher salt
Pinch ground cinnamon

Toast the sesame seeds on the stove top in a dry skillet over medium heat, shaking them frequently to avoid burning, until they are fragrant and just a shade darker (3–5 minutes). Combine all the ingredients in a small bowl and mix well. Stored in an airtight container in a cool, dark place, this dry rub will keep for a month.

Dill-Pomegranate Butter

MARJORAM-GRILLED LAMB WITH ARUGULA, LIMA BEANS, AND PORT-MUSTARD DRESSING

Marjoram is an underappreciated herb, with a more dynamic flavor than many of its better-known cousins. Here we use it with lamb, for which it has a particular affinity. The accompanying lima bean and arugula salad is a tribute to Chris's mom, who always served lima beans with her lamb chops. (If you have any dressing left over, don't throw it out—it's delicious drizzled over any kind of red meat, hot or cold.)

Serves 4 as a salad course or appetizer

THE SALAD

1 lb (450g) boneless lamb sirloin
¼ cup olive oil
1 teaspoon minced garlic
2 tablespoons roughly chopped fresh marjoram (or substitute oregano)
Kosher salt and freshly cracked black pepper
2 bunches arugula, trimmed, washed, and dried well
1 cup cooked fresh lima beans, or 1 cup frozen lima beans, thawed

THE DRESSING

1 tablespoon Dijon mustard
1 teaspoon minced shallot
2 tablespoons port
⅓ cup extra virgin olive oil
Kosher salt and freshly cracked black pepper to taste

Build a multilevel fire in your grill (see p31). When the coals are all ignited, the flames have died down, and the temperature is hot (see p34), you're ready to cook.

Dry the lamb well with paper towels. Combine the oil, garlic, and marjoram in a small bowl, and mix well. Rub the lamb all over with this mixture, then sprinkle generously with salt and pepper. Place the lamb on the hot side of the grill and sear well (about 10 minutes per side). Move to the medium-hot area of the grill and continue to cook until the meat reaches the internal temperature you like (4–6 minutes per side for medium-rare). To check for doneness, insert a meat thermometer into the dead center of the roast, let it sit for 5 seconds, then read the temperature: you're looking for 120°F (49°C) for rare, 126°F (52°C) for medium-rare (how we like it), 134°F (57°C) for medium, 150°F (66°C) for medium-well, and 160°F (70°C) for well done. Remove the lamb from the grill, cover loosely with foil, and let it rest for 10 minutes.

While the lamb is resting, make the salad: Combine the arugula and lima beans in a large bowl. In a small bowl, whisk together the mustard, shallots, and port; add the oil slowly in a thin stream, whisking until well blended. Season with salt and pepper, then drizzle the beans and arugula with just enough dressing to coat lightly, and toss well. Divide among four salad plates.

Slice the lamb against the grain, ¼–½ in (0.5–1cm) thick. Fan ¼ of the slices over each salad, drizzle with a little more dressing, and serve.

SIDES AND SNACKS

SO-CALLED "SIDE DISHES" CAN BE AS ENTICING AND SATISYING AS ANY ENTRÉE. AND IF YOU'RE A VEGETARIAN, THIS IS THE CHAPTER FOR YOU: PUT TWO OR THREE OF THESE DISHES TOGETHER, AND YOU'VE GOT A GRILLED MEAL THAT WILL HAVE YOU WONDERING WHERE FLAMES HAVE BEEN ALL YOUR LIFE.

GRILL BREAD

We love grilled bread. Not only is it a great accompaniment to any meal, it also makes a wonderful appetizer when drizzled with some flavored oil or dipped into a relish or salsa. Of course, you can always use store-bought bread, but it's more fun to make your own. Plus it always tastes better. Plus your guests are always impressed. This is a pretty standard flatbread recipe with some added beer for flavor and cornmeal for texture, which makes it particularly good for the grill. When it comes off the coals, hot and slightly charred with its delightful crunch and its delicious yeasty taste, you'll be a hero.

Makes 4 flat loaves

THE INGREDIENTS

1 tablespoon active dry yeast
3 cups all-purpose flour, divided
½ cup warm water
2 tablespoons olive oil, plus more for brushing

½ cup beer of your choice, at room temperature
¼ cup yellow cornmeal, plus more for dusting
1 teaspoon kosher salt, plus more for sprinkling

Stir together the yeast and ½ cup flour in the bowl of an electric mixer. Add the warm water and mix until just blended. Cover with a damp towel and let stand in a warm, draft-free place (inside a gas oven with the pilot light on, for example) for 30 minutes, until the mixture is thick and foamy and gives off a sound sort of like soda fizz when you stir it.

Add 2 tablespoons of oil and the beer to the yeast mixture and mix well. Add the cornmeal and 1 teaspoon salt, and begin adding the remaining 2½ cups of flour, ½ cup at a time, to form a soft dough (you may not need all of the flour). Turn the dough out onto a floured board and knead, adding as much of the remaining flour as necessary to prevent the dough from sticking, until the dough is satiny and just slightly sticky (about 8 minutes).

Place the dough in an oiled bowl, turning once to coat. Cover loosely and let rise in a warm place until it has doubled in bulk (1–1½ hours). Divide the dough into quarters and form each piece into a ball. Sprinkle a baking sheet with cornmeal and put the balls of dough on the sheet, then cover loosely and let rise again for 30 minutes. (At this point, you can cover the dough with plastic wrap and refrigerate it until about an hour before you want to grill the bread.)

Build a fire in your grill. When the coals are all ignited, the flames have died down, and the temperature is medium (*see p34*), you're ready to cook.

Stretch each ball of dough into a rough circle or rectangle about ⅛in (3mm) thick and 10in (25cm) across. Brush with additional olive oil and sprinkle with salt, then place it directly on the grill and cook until black spots form on the bottom and bubbles form on the top (about 4 minutes). Flip the bread over and grill the other side until golden and crusty (3–4 minutes more). Remove from the grill and serve right away.

FLAVORED OILS FOR GRILL BREAD

When your bread comes hot off the grill (*see previous page*), drizzle it with one of these oils and set it out along with the rest of the oil for dipping, and you've got a spectacular, slightly unusual appetizer. These oils will all keep for up to a week, covered and refrigerated. But since the oil will partially congeal when it's cold, remember to let it sit out to re-liquefy for about 15 minutes before serving.

ROAST GARLIC AND MARJORAM OIL

Makes about ¾ cup

1 head garlic
½ cup extra virgin olive oil, divided
2 teaspoons kosher salt
1 teaspoon cracked black pepper
2 tablespoons roughly chopped fresh marjoram
Kosher salt and freshly cracked black pepper to taste

Slice the top quarter off the head of garlic, put it in a bowl with ¼ cup of the olive oil, salt, and pepper, and toss gently to combine. Wrap the garlic securely in 2 large sheets of heavy-duty foil.

Ash-roast or oven-braise the garlic: Either place the package in the coals around the periphery of a fire, where the heat is less intense, or in an oven preheated to 300°F (150°C). Cook until the garlic feels soft when pressed through the foil (about 1 hour in the oven, or 30 minutes in the fire).

Remove the pack from the fire or oven, cut the foil open, and wait until the garlic is cool enough to handle before squeezing the flesh from each clove.

Combine the garlic, the remaining olive oil, marjoram, and salt and pepper in a bowl and mix together well.

SPICY CUMIN AND ORANGE OIL

Makes about ¾ cup

½ cup extra virgin olive oil
2 tablespoons cumin seeds, freshly cracked
2 tablespoons roughly chopped fresh oregano
1 tablespoon finely minced orange zest
1 teaspoon red pepper flakes
Kosher salt and freshly cracked black pepper to taste

Combine all the ingredients in a small saucepan and warm over medium-low heat for 15 minutes. Let cool to room temperature before using.

SUN-DRIED TOMATO AND BASIL OIL

Makes about 1 cup

½ cup extra virgin olive oil
¼ cup roughly chopped oil-packed sun-dried tomatoes
¼ cup lightly packed julienned fresh basil leaves
1 teaspoon minced fresh garlic
Kosher salt and freshly cracked black pepper to taste

Combine all the ingredients in a bowl and mix well. Allow to sit for at least 30 minutes before serving, so the tomatoes become lush and soft.

MEDITERRANEAN CHOPPED SALAD
ON GRILL BREAD

This chopped salad is a good accompaniment to a grilled meal all by itself. But arranged on top of rounds of home-grilled bread, it makes a substantial appetizer that works perfectly in front of a simple grilled seafood entrée. It's also a very satisfying light lunch on a hot day, along with a glass of rosé and a rich dessert like grilled banana upside-down cake (*see p322*). If you want to make it easy on yourself, buy pre-pitted olives for this one.

Serves 4 to 8 as an appetizer

THE INGREDIENTS

1 recipe Grill Bread (*see p270*), shaped into 4 rounds
   but not cooked
3 tablespoons extra virgin olive oil
2 tomatoes, about the size of baseballs, cored,
   seeded, and diced small
2 cucumbers, halved, seeded, and diced small
½ cup brine-cured black olives, such as kalamata,
   pitted and roughly chopped
½ cup roughly chopped fresh parsley
⅓ cup extra virgin olive oil
¼ cup red wine vinegar
½ cup crumbled feta cheese
Kosher salt and freshly cracked black pepper to taste

Build a fire in your grill. When the coals are all ignited, the flames have died down, and the temperature is medium (*see p34*), you're ready to cook.

Brush the bread rounds with oil on both sides, then place on the grill directly over the coals and cook until nicely toasted and brown on one side (about 4 minutes). Flip the bread over and grill the other side until golden and crusty (3–4 minutes more).

While the bread is on the grill, combine the tomatoes, cucumbers, olives, and parsley in a bowl. Whisk together the oil and vinegar in another bowl, then add just enough dressing to moisten the salad, tossing gently until evenly mixed.

Place a grilled bread round on each salad plate. At the last minute, toss the feta cheese with the tomato salad and season with salt and pepper. Top each bread round with a portion of the salad and serve.

CUCUMBERS WITH MINT, CUMIN, AND YOGURT WITH GRILL BREAD

This Greek-style mixture is a wonderful dipping sauce for grilled bread. For the best flavor and texture, use Greek whole-milk yogurt. If you want to be a bit more formal, you can also serve this as a sit-down appetizer, with the cucumber mixture spooned generously over the rounds of bread.

Serves 4 as an appetizer

THE INGREDIENTS

1 recipe Grill Bread (*see p270*), shaped into 4 rounds
   but not cooked
3 tablespoons extra virgin olive oil
½ cucumber, peeled if desired, diced small
   (about 1 cup)
½ cup plain yogurt
3 tablespoons roughly chopped fresh mint
1 tablespoon fresh lemon juice
1 tablespoon ground cumin
Kosher salt and freshly cracked black pepper to taste

Build a fire in your grill. When the coals are all ignited, the flames have died down, and the temperature is medium (*see p34*), you're ready to cook.

Brush the bread rounds with oil on both sides, then place on the grill directly over the coals and cook until nicely toasted and brown on one side (about 4 minutes). Flip the bread over and grill the other side until golden and crusty (3–4 minutes more).

While the bread is on the grill, combine the cucumber, yogurt, mint, lemon juice, cumin, and salt and pepper in a bowl and mix well.

Cut the bread into wedges or just set it out so people can tear a piece and spoon the yogurt relish on top.

BLUE CHEESE, PEAR, AND CARAMELIZED ONION PIZZAS

Putting a foil pan over food on the grill creates a sort of mini-oven. It's a useful strategy for cooking thick cuts of meat all the way through without burning them on the outside. Here we use this approach to melt blue cheese on grill bread without putting it over a fire so hot that it would burn the dough on the bottom.

Serves 4 to 6 as an appetizer

THE INGREDIENTS

6 tablespoons extra virgin olive oil, divided
3 red onions, peeled and sliced into thin rings
Kosher salt and freshly cracked black pepper to taste
1 recipe Grill Bread (*see p270*), shaped into 4 rounds
    but not cooked
2 ripe but firm pears, cored and sliced thin
½ cup crumbled blue cheese of your choice
¼ cup roughly chopped fresh parsley

On the stove top, heat 3 tablespoons of the extra virgin olive oil in a large sauté pan or skillet over medium heat until it is hot but not smoking. Add the onions, sprinkle with salt and pepper, and sauté, stirring occasionally, until the onions start to soften (about 5 minutes). Reduce the heat to low and continue to cook, stirring often, until the onions are well caramelized (20–30 minutes).

While the onions are cooking, build a fire in your grill. When the coals are all ignited, the flames have died down, and the temperature is medium (*see p34*), you're ready to cook.

When the onions are ready, brush the bread rounds on both sides with the remaining 3 tablespoons oil, then place on the grill directly over the coals and cook until nicely toasted and brown on one side (about 4 minutes). Flip the bread over and top each round with a pile of caramelized onions, then arrange the pear slices over the onions and scatter the blue cheese on top. Invert a foil pan over the pizzas and continue to cook until the cheese starts to melt (3–4 minutes more).

Cut the pizzas into wedges with a large, sharp knife, arrange on a platter, sprinkle with parsley, and serve.

PEACH, PARMESAN, AND CRISP PROSCIUTTO PIZZAS

Fruit on grill bread might seem like an odd idea, but this combination of sweet, lush peaches, nutty parmesan, and rich, salty prosciutto will win you over. Be careful not to leave the prosciutto over the coals too long; you don't need to cook it, you just want to crisp it up and give it a little smokiness.

Serves 4 to 6 as an appetizer

THE INGREDIENTS

6oz (175g) very thinly sliced prosciutto
¼ cup extra virgin olive oil
1 teaspoon minced fresh garlic
1 recipe Grill Bread (*see p270*), shaped into 4 rounds
　but not cooked
2 ripe but firm peaches, halved, pitted, and sliced thin
¾ cup grated parmesan cheese
2 tablespoons roughly chopped fresh basil

Build a fire in your grill. When the coals are all ignited, the flames have died down, and the temperature is medium (*see p34*), you're ready to cook.

Put the prosciutto slices on the grill directly over the coals and cook until just crisp (about 1 minute). Set aside.

Combine the olive oil and garlic in a small bowl and mix well. Brush the bread rounds on both sides with garlic oil, then place on the grill directly over the coals and cook until nicely toasted and brown on one side (about 4 minutes). Flip the bread over and arrange the grilled prosciutto and some of the peach slices on each one. Season lightly with salt and pepper and scatter the cheese on top, then invert a foil pan over the pizzas and continue to cook until the cheese starts to melt (3–4 minutes more).

Cut the pizzas into wedges with a large, sharp knife, drizzle with some of the remaining garlic oil, then arrange on a platter, sprinkle with basil, and serve.

GRILLED SHRIMP, BACON, AND ASIAGO PIZZAS

We figure that most any combination we like in general, we'll also like on top of our grill bread. Since we love shrimp, bacon, and cheese—I mean, really, who doesn't?—we decided to give it a try. It turned out to be one of our top favorite pizza choices, and everyone else we've tried it out on has been equally enthusiastic.

Serves 4 to 6 as an appetizer

THE INGREDIENTS

12 medium-large (16/20) shrimp, peeled, deveined, and halved lengthwise

6 slices bacon, diced small

4 tablespoons extra virgin olive oil, divided

2 tablespoons roughly chopped fresh thyme

Kosher salt and freshly cracked black pepper to taste

1 recipe Grill Bread (*see p270*), shaped into 4 rounds but not cooked

1 cup grated Asiago or other hard Italian cheese, such as Parmigiano Reggiano

On the stove top, cook the bacon in a sauté pan over medium heat until crisp (6–8 minutes). Drain well.

Build a fire in your grill. When the coals are all ignited, the flames have died down, and the temperature is medium (*see p34*), you're ready to cook.

Combine the shrimp, bacon, 1 tablespoon of the olive oil, thyme, and salt and pepper in a bowl and mix until the shrimp and bacon are evenly coated.

Brush the bread rounds on both sides with the remaining 3 tablespoons of olive oil, then place them on the grill directly over the coals and cook until nicely toasted and brown on one side (about 4 minutes). Flip the bread over and top each round with some of the shrimp mixture, then scatter the cheese on top. Invert a foil pan over the pizzas, and continue to cook until the shrimp are just cooked through and the cheese is starting to melt (3–4 minutes more).

Cut the pizzas into wedges with a large, sharp knife. Arrange on a platter, and serve.

GRILLED NEW POTATOES WITH ROSEMARY, GARLIC, AND BLACK OLIVES

We're strongly in favor of anything that puts a nice, brown crust on a potato. Here we use live fire to do it, which also gives the potatoes a lovely slightly smoky taste. Before the potatoes go on the grill, we parboil them (to ensure they cook all the way through over the fire), then when they come off the grill, we coat them with Italian flavorings.

Serves 4 as a side dish

THE INGREDIENTS

20 small new potatoes (or 10 larger ones, halved), well washed

3 tablespoons vegetable oil

2 tablespoons minced garlic

Kosher salt and freshly cracked black pepper to taste

¼ cup roughly chopped pitted kalamata or other brine-cured black olives

¼ cup extra virgin olive oil

Juice of 1 lemon (about ¼ cup)

2 tablespoons roughly chopped fresh rosemary

Kosher salt and freshly cracked black pepper to taste

On the stove top, bring a pot of salted water to a boil and cook the potatoes, uncovered, just until they can be pierced easily with a fork but still offer some resistance (6–8 minutes). Immediately plunge them into ice water to stop the cooking, drain well, and refrigerate until cold.

Build a fire in your grill. When the coals are all ignited, the flames have died down, and the temperature is medium (*see p34*), you're ready to cook.

Put the chilled potatoes in a large bowl. Add the vegetable oil, garlic, and salt and pepper and toss gently until the potatoes are evenly coated. Thread the potatoes onto skewers; if they are halved, put each half facing the same way so that the cut sides lie flat. Arrange the skewers on the grill over the coals and cook until the potatoes are golden brown (3–4 minutes). Flip over and cook for 2 minutes more.

When the potatoes are done, carefully push them off the skewers back into the same large bowl. Add the olives, olive oil, lemon juice, rosemary, and salt and pepper to taste, and toss gently until the potatoes are evenly coated. Transfer to a serving dish and serve immediately.

SIMPLE GRILLED BALSAMIC RED ONIONS WITH BASIL AND PARMESAN

This easy side dish is ideal for anyone who loves Italian flavors and grilled onions—and that's a very wide group indeed. Add that to the fact that it takes next to no time to prepare, and you have a dish with nearly universal appeal. Cut the onion rings nice and thick, and they'll be less likely to fall apart on the grill.

Serves 4 to 6 as a side dish

THE INGREDIENTS

2 large red onions, peeled and sliced into rings about
    1in (2.5cm) thick
2 tablespoons vegetable oil
Kosher salt and freshly cracked black pepper
¼ cup extra virgin olive oil
¼ cup balsamic vinegar
¼ cup thinly sliced fresh basil leaves
¼ cup grated parmesan cheese

Build a fire in your grill. When the coals are all ignited, the flames have died down, and the temperature is medium (*see p34*), you're ready to cook.

Rub the onion slices with the vegetable oil, keeping the rings together. Sprinkle the onions generously with salt and pepper. Put them on the grill directly over the coals and cook until soft and golden brown—about 10 minutes per side.

When the onions are done, transfer them to a medium-sized bowl and add the olive oil, vinegar, basil, and parmesan, tossing to separate the onion slices into rings and incorporate all of the ingredients.

Pile the grilled onions on a serving platter and drizzle generously with the remaining dressing.

MORE SIMPLE GRILLED VEGETABLES

With your fire temperature at medium (*see p34*), you can treat your guests to a tasty selection of grilled vegetables. The red bell peppers below would team perfectly with the grilled onions opposite (*see also overleaf*) to accompany any Mediterranean-style main dish—or, if your meal has more of an Asian flavor, try the eggplant and zucchini recipes. Each serves 4–6 people as a side dish.

GRILLED RED PEPPERS WITH PARSLEY-PINE NUT CONDIMENT

5 red bell peppers, halved, cored, and seeded
¼ cup olive or vegetable oil
Kosher salt and freshly cracked black pepper
1 recipe Parsley-Pine Nut Condiment (*see p262*)

Rub the pepper halves lightly with oil and sprinkle them generously with salt and pepper, then put them on the grill directly over the coals and cook until they are golden brown but still crisp (2–3 minutes per side). When the peppers are done, cut them into thin strips and transfer them to a large bowl. Add the condiment to the peppers and toss until evenly mixed. Pile the peppers on a platter and serve immediately.

GRILLED EGGPLANT WITH GINGER-SOY BARBECUE SAUCE

1 large eggplant, cut into slices about 1in (2.5cm) thick
3 tablespoons olive oil
Kosher salt and freshly cracked black pepper
1 recipe Ginger-Soy Barbecue Sauce (*see p228*)

Rub the eggplant slices on both sides with the oil and sprinkle generously with salt and pepper, then put them on the grill directly over the coals and cook, turning once, until the interior is tender and moist all the way through (3–4 minutes per side). Brush with the barbecue sauce during the last 30 seconds of cooking on each side. Transfer the eggplant slices to a serving platter and serve, passing the remaining barbecue sauce on the side.

ASIAN-STYLE GRILLED ZUCCHINI

4 medium zucchini, halved lengthwise to make 8 planks about 1in (2.5cm) thick
1 recipe Sesame-Ginger Paste (*see p231*)
Kosher salt

Rub the zucchini planks generously with the sesame paste and sprinkle them lightly with salt, then put them on the grill and cook, turning once, until the zucchini looks moist all the way through and the interior has lost its raw, opaque look (3–4 minutes per side). Transfer the zucchini to a platter and serve.

GRILLED CORN

There's nothing better than fresh sweet corn on the grill. Because it's so popular, people have developed many ways of cooking it. We provide three here: They all make sense to us, because each has its own virtues. Whichever method you choose to use, our Latin Flavor Modifiers (*see overleaf*) are the perfect accompaniment to the end result.

Allow 1 ear of corn per person

FIRST METHOD: HUSK-ON AND SOAKED

This is a good method to use if you are a big fan of tenderness in your corn, but aren't too concerned with time.

Soak the ears in water for 15 minutes.

Place the ears on the grill over a medium fire (*see p34*) and let them steam until they are just cooked through (about 15–20 minutes). To check for doneness, peel back the husk on one ear and poke the kernels to be sure they are tender.

Remove the husks and silk, brush on a little butter, season with salt and pepper, then roll the ears around on the grill ever so slightly to add a little char.

SECOND METHOD: NAKED CORN

This is a good everyday approach to grilling corn: It's easy, it's quick, and you get good corn flavor plus a nice smokiness.

Shuck and de-silk the ears.

Place the ears over a medium-low fire (*see p34*) and let them cook for 3–5 minutes, rolling them around for even cooking, until they are just golden brown. To check for doneness, poke the kernels to be sure they are tender.

THIRD METHOD: ASH-ROASTED

This is probably our favorite approach—not only does it produce very smoky-flavored corn, but it also allows you to cook it with some of the butter, salt, and pepper already on it.

Shuck and de-silk the ears of corn.

Wrap each ear, along with butter, salt, and pepper to your liking, in a double layer of foil. Put the packages in the coals of your grill fire for 12–15 minutes. To check for doneness, peel open one of the packages and poke at the kernels to be sure they are tender.

Remove the corn from the foil packages, brush on more butter, season with more salt and pepper to taste, and serve.

LATIN FLAVOR MODIFIERS FOR CORN

These bursts of flavor with a citrus twist are particularly welcome at the height of corn season, when you want grilled corn (*see pp288–9*) with every meal but are looking for a little variety in how you serve it. Each of these should be enough for a dozen or more ears.

ORANGE-CHIPOTLE BUTTER

½ cup orange juice
2 tablespoons minced chipotle peppers in adobo sauce
½ cup unsalted butter, softened

On the stove top, bring the orange juice to a boil in a small saucepan over high heat. Reduce the heat to medium-low and simmer vigorously until reduced by two-thirds in volume (15–20 minutes). Remove the pan from the heat, stir in the chipotles, and let cool to room temperature. When cooled, add to the butter and mash it all together well. Top each ear of hot grilled corn with a generous helping of the butter. (Any leftover butter can be wrapped in wax paper and refrigerated; it will keep for up to 3 days.)

CUMIN SALT WITH LIME

½ cup kosher salt
¼ cup cumin seeds
3 limes, cut into wedges

Combine the salt and cumin seeds in a small sauté pan over low heat. Cook, stirring constantly, until the seeds start to smoke slightly and become fragrant (2–3 minutes). Set aside. Squeeze the lime wedges over the grilled corn, then sprinkle liberally with the flavored salt.

CILANTRO-LIME BUTTER

¼ cup roughly chopped fresh cilantro
Juice of 1 lime (about 2 tablespoons)
1 tablespoon chile powder
½ cup unsalted butter, softened

Work the cilantro, lime juice, and chile powder into the butter in a small bowl, mixing well. You can use the butter right away, or wrap it in plastic wrap, shape it into a square log, and refrigerate until firm.

When you're ready to serve the corn, place the butter, unwrapped, in a shallow dish. Let your guests roll their own corn on the butter (the way most people do at home when they eat corn on the cob and no one's watching).

MALAYSIA: FOOD FANTASY

To put it mildly, we were not thrilled to be stranded overnight in the gritty truck-stop town of Johor Bahru, Malaysia. But, figuring we might as well make the best of it, we decided to check out the local open-air market.

The moment we walked in, our overnight stay began to seem less a delay than a delight. We wandered past stalls featuring frogs' legs, boar snouts, and huge piles of greens whose names we didn't know, then browsed the seafood section, where giant eels, cockles, spiny lobsters, and four types of crabs lay on glistening rows of ice. Next we hit the fruit stands, crowded with specimens that seemed too bizarre to be real: Red-orange rambutans, bristling with pointy spikes; purple-brown mangosteens, the white inner flesh tasting of molasses, lemon, and cream; beadlike chiku, gooey and sweet as boiled frosting; huge orange-yellow jackfruit, mealy and mellow, hinting of vanilla. Other fruits, like mango and papaya, were familiar in form, but had flavors of a depth and complexity we had never experienced. When we walked back to the hotel at dusk, we discovered that the parking lot had been transformed into a hawker center, with dozens of bicycle-propelled food stands arranged around a handful of folding tables and chairs. Excited, we joined the crowd and sampled dish after dish—stingray tail dabbed with hot sauce, wrapped in a banana leaf, and roasted in hot coals; plump and satisfyingly fatty curried frogs' legs; water greens sautéed with chiles and garlic. Instead of dessert, we ordered what looked like a fruit salad, rich with the variety we had seen earlier at the market. It was a classic example of Malay food, the sweet, fecund intensity of the fruits perfectly complemented by a peanut sauce laced with chiles and a hint of *belacan*, their beloved fermented shrimp paste. The moral, it seemed, was clear: Never underestimate a truck stop.

TROPICAL FRUIT SALAD
WITH SPICY LIME-PEANUT DRESSING

Inspired by Malaysian rojak, this is a fruit salad with a bit of savory/spicy attitude. If you want to make this more authentic and have access to (and a taste for) the shrimp paste called *belacan*, add a teaspoon or so to the dressing. Although native to the Americas, the jicama is very popular in Asian cuisines. It's sometimes called the Mexican potato, which does little justice to its juicy crispness and sweet taste. If you can't find jicama, use a crisp green apple or Asian pear instead.

Serves 4 as a side dish

1 mango, pitted, peeled, and diced medium
1 papaya, seeded, peeled, and diced medium
½ cup medium diced pineapple
½ cup medium diced jicama
¼ cup roughly chopped fresh cilantro

For the dressing:
¼ cup roughly chopped roasted unsalted peanuts
1 tablespoon minced fresh ginger
1 tablespooon minced red or green fresh chile pepper of your choice
Juice of 2 limes (about ¼ cup)
2 tablespoons soy sauce
1 tablespoon soft dark brown sugar

Combine all the fruits and the cilantro in a large bowl.

Combine all the dressing ingredients in a small bowl and whisk until well blended.

Add just enough of the dressing to the fruit mixture to moisten, toss gently, and serve.

WAY HOT CHILE-RUBBED GRILLED SUMMER SQUASH

We like the mild flavor of summer squash, but lots of our friends complain that it's a little boring. Well, this one is for them. The paste that we coat the squash planks with during the last minute of cooking is hot and intense with dried chiles and other deep flavors. Pass a bowl of it around separately when you serve this, in case your daredevil friends want more.

Serves 4 to 6 as a side dish

THE SQUASH

4 medium summer squash, unpeeled, halved lengthwise to make 8 planks about 1in (2.5cm) thick

2 tablespoons olive oil
Kosher salt and freshly cracked black pepper

THE CHILE PASTE

¼ cup crushed ancho chiles or other dried chiles of your choice
¼ cup roughly chopped fresh cilantro
¼ cup olive oil
2 tablespoons cumin seeds
Juice of 1 lime (about 2 tablespoons)
1 tablespoon minced fresh garlic
1 tablespoon kosher salt
1 tablespoon freshly cracked black pepper

Build a fire in your grill. When the coals are all ignited, the flames have died down, and the temperature is medium (*see p34*), you're ready to cook.

Combine all the chile paste ingredients in a small bowl, mix well, and set aside.

Rub the squash planks lightly on both sides with oil and sprinkle them generously with salt and pepper, then put them on the grill directly over the coals and cook, turning once, until the interior is moist all the way through and has lost its raw, opaque look (3–4 minutes per side). Brush them with the chile paste during the last minute of cooking.

Arrange the squash planks on a platter and serve warm or at room temperature. Pass the remaining chile paste separately so that fire-eaters can add more.

GRILLED POTATO STEAKS
WITH BACON AND SOUR CREAM

Who doesn't love a baked potato with the works—butter, sour cream, bacon, and chives? Here we go that classic combo one better by slicing the potatoes into thick planks, which we like to call "steaks," then grilling them before piling on the extras. This is the side dish to make when you're having a grilled steak dinner.

Serves 4

THE INGREDIENTS

2 large baking potatoes, well scrubbed (not peeled)
4 slices bacon, diced small
2 tablespoons olive oil
Kosher salt and freshly cracked black pepper to taste
½ cup sour cream
1 small bunch chives, minced
¼ cup unsalted butter (optional)

Build a fire in your grill. When the coals are all ignited, the flames have died down, and the temperature is medium (*see p34*), you're ready to cook.

While you wait for the fire, cut thin slices lengthwise off 2 parallel sides of each potato so you can lay them flat. Now cut each potato in half lengthwise to make 2 steaks, each 1–1½in (about 3cm) thick.

On the stove top, bring a large pan of boiling salted water to a boil and reduce the heat to a gentle simmer. Cook the potatoes gently in the simmering water until just done but still very firm (8–9 minutes). To check for doneness, poke with a toothpick: It should slide into the potato, but meet with a fair amount of resistance. Drain the potatoes and pat them dry with paper towels.

Meanwhile, cook the bacon in a small sauté pan or skillet over medium heat until crisp (6–8 minutes), then transfer to kitchen paper to drain.

Brush the potato steaks with oil and sprinkle them generously with salt and pepper, then put them on the grill directly over the coals and cook, turning once, until they are really crispy and brown (4–5 minutes per side).

Arrange the potatoes on a platter and top with the bacon, sour cream, and chives, plus the butter if desired.

GRILLED BROCCOLI WITH LEMON BUTTER

We are big fans of broccoli, so we're always looking for new ways to cook it. This rather novel approach—dividing the bunch into quarters, blanching it, then giving it a nice gentle char on the grill before mixing it with butter and lemon juice—adds an appealing smoky dimension to an old favorite.

Serves 4 as a side dish

THE INGREDIENTS

1 large bunch broccoli, sliced lengthwise into quarters

Kosher salt and freshly cracked black pepper

3 tablespoons olive oil

½ cup unsalted butter, softened

Juice of ½ lemon (about 2 tablespoons)

Build a fire in your grill. When the coals are all ignited, the flames have died down, and the temperature is medium (*see p34*), you're ready to cook.

While you wait for the fire to reach cooking temperature, on the stove top, bring a pan of salted water to a boil. Blanch the broccoli quarters for 1 minute, then drain well.

Put the blanched broccoli in a large bowl, sprinkle it generously with salt and pepper, drizzle it with the oil, and toss to coat. Put the broccoli on the grill directly over the coals and cook until tender (2–3 minutes per side), then return to the same large bowl.

Add the butter, lemon juice, and more salt and pepper to taste to the hot broccoli, tossing gently to coat. Transfer to a serving dish and serve immediately.

SOUTHEAST ASIAN-STYLE GRILLED ZUCCHINI

Gardeners often complain about having too much zucchini, but we love it. It's a supremely adaptable vegetable, easily paired with all kinds of flavor footprints, like the Southeast Asian barbecue sauce we brush on it in this dish. Cutting the zucchini into planks makes it easy to grill them to tenderness without burning the outside.

Serves 4 as a side dish

THE INGREDIENTS

4 medium zucchini, unpeeled, halved lengthwise to make 8 planks about 1in (2.5cm) thick

2 tablespoons Asian sesame oil

Kosher salt and freshly cracked white pepper to taste (or substitute black pepper)

1 recipe Mango-Chile Barbecue Sauce (*see p210*)

Build a fire in your grill. When the coals are all ignited, the flames have died down, and the temperature is medium (*see p34*), you're ready to cook.

Rub the zucchini planks lightly on both sides with sesame oil and sprinkle them generously with salt and pepper, then put them on the grill directly over the coals and cook, turning once, until the interior is moist all the way through and has lost its raw, opaque look (3–4 minutes per side).

Add the grilled zucchini to the bowl of barbecue sauce and toss gently to coat. Transfer to a serving platter and serve warm or at room temperature.

EGGPLANT AND TOMATO HOBO PACK

If you want to make delicious, slightly unusual side dishes without a lot of work, hobo packs (*see p19*) are for you. Just assemble the foil package, slide it into the coals, and let it cook while you make the rest of the meal on top of the grill grid. This combination of eggplant and tomatoes is a classic pairing found throughout the Mediterranean world, and for good reason—the rich eggplant and sweet-tart tomato complement each other perfectly. Add a little garlic, onion, oregano, and hot pepper, and you've got a super-tasty side dish that goes with just about any meal. It's also a delicious vegetarian entrée for two.

Serves 4 as a side dish

THE INGREDIENTS

2 small eggplants, unpeeled, cut into 2in (5cm) cubes
2 tomatoes about the size of baseballs, cored and
  diced large
1 red onion, peeled and diced large
5 peeled garlic cloves
⅓ cup extra virgin olive oil
2 tablespoons roughly chopped fresh oregano
1 teaspoon red pepper flakes
Kosher salt and freshly cracked black pepper to taste

Combine all the ingredients in a large bowl and toss gently until evenly mixed.

Tear off 4 sheets of heavy-duty foil, each about 2ft (60cm) long, and stack them one on top of the other. Arrange the vegetables in the center of the top sheet.

Fold up the sheets around the ingredients, one after another, turning the package one-quarter turn between each sheet and making sure that each sheet is well sealed around the food. If necessary, divide the ingredients in half and make 2 hobo packs. Or, place the ingredients in a deep disposable foil pan (*see overleaf*) and cover tightly with a double layer of heavy-duty foil.

Place the hobo pack (or packs) in the coals around the periphery of the fire, where the heat is less intense. Pile the coals up around the pack and cook until the eggplant is cooked through (20–30 minutes).

Remove the pack from the coals and unwrap the foil; if the vegetables need more time, put it back in the coals or in a 300°F (150°C) oven until it's done.

MORE HOBO PACK COMBINATIONS

All kinds of vegetables and fruits can be cooked using the hobo pack method. It's a great way to cook corn, for example (*see p288*)—and we also use it for some fantastic desserts (*see pp318–9*). You can cook individual vegetables with just a little butter or olive oil, salt, and pepper, or experiment with combinations—the approach we prefer. Here's a quartet of our favorites. For each, follow exactly the same method as on the page opposite. Each recipe serves 4 as a side dish.

NEW POTATOES AND GARLIC

Potatoes, garlic, and onion form one of those combinations that makes your mouth water any time you smell it cooking. It's even better when it has a little edge of smoke from cooking in the coals. This is a wonderful side dish with a big, juicy grilled steak.

16 new potatoes about the size of golf balls, scrubbed but not peeled

1 red onion, peeled and diced large

1 large head garlic, separated into cloves and peeled

¼ cup olive oil

Kosher salt and freshly cracked black pepper to taste

SWEET POTATO AND GREEN GRAPE

When you unwrap the foil from this combo, the rich, moist sweet potatoes flavored with smoke, sage, and brown sugar and complemented by the sweetness of the grapes will be a revelation.

2 sweet potatoes, peeled and diced large

1 cup green grapes

Juice of 1 lemon (about ¼ cup)

¼ cup extra virgin olive oil

9 roughly chopped fresh sage leaves

1 tablespoon soft dark brown sugar

Kosher salt and freshly cracked black pepper to taste

MUSHROOM AND PEARL ONION

There's no reason to save pearl onions for Thanksgiving. Combined with mushrooms, butter, parsley, and a dash of sherry, they make a delicious and versatile side dish. If you feel like laying out a little more cash, wild mushrooms take this dish to an even higher level.

1lb (450g) white mushrooms, stems trimmed

12 pearl onions about the size of golf balls, trimmed but not peeled, and minced

½ cup chilled unsalted butter, diced

¼ cup roughly chopped fresh parsley

2 tablespoons dry sherry

Kosher salt and freshly cracked black pepper to taste

POTATO AND LEEK

Vichyssoise may be the best-known pairing of potatoes and leeks, but they are also wonderful together in this simple but rather elegant hobo pack. Be sure to wash the leeks well; the best way is to halve them lengthwise and then immerse them for several minutes in a sink of cold water, then rinse twice in cold running water.

2 large baking potatoes, scrubbed well and diced large

4 medium leeks, white parts only, trimmed, very well washed, and sliced thin

½ cup roughly chopped scallions, with green tops

½ cup chilled unsalted butter, diced

Kosher salt and freshly cracked black pepper to taste

MAPLE-GLAZED GRILLED SWEET POTATOES

Sweet potatoes have a wonderful earthy sweetness that is beautifully enhanced by a little char from the grill. Glazed with a simple maple syrup-butter combination, they are a fantastic side dish for just about any grilled meal, particularly in early autumn. We are especially fond of them with the grilled veal chops on p56, or the pheasant breasts on p170.

Serves 4 as a side dish

THE INGREDIENTS

3 sweet potatoes, peeled and cut on the bias into
    slices about 1in (2.5cm) thick
⅓ cup maple syrup
⅓ cup unsalted butter
2 tablespoons olive oil
Kosher salt and freshly cracked black pepper

Build a fire in your grill. When the coals are all ignited, the flames have died down, and the temperature is medium (*see p34*), you're ready to cook.

On the stove top, bring a large pan of boiling salted water to the boil and reduce the heat to a gentle simmer. Cook the sweet potato slices gently in the simmering water until just tender but still very firm (6–8 minutes). To check for doneness, poke one of the slices with a toothpick: It should slide in, but still meet with a fair amount of resistance. Drain the slices and pat them dry with paper towels.

Combine the maple syrup and butter in a small saucepan over medium heat, stirring occasionally, until the butter melts. Remove from the heat and set aside.

Brush the potatoes with oil and sprinkle them generously with salt and pepper, then put them on the grill directly over the coals and cook, turning once, until they are nicely browned and tender (3–4 minutes per side). Brush the potatoes with the syrup mixture during the last minute of cooking on each side. Serve hot or at room temperature, drizzled with a bit more of the syrup mixture.

GRILLED WHITE MUSHROOMS
WITH BACON AND PARMESAN

Oh, yeah, oh, yeah. This is one of the great side dishes of the grilled repertoire. It's rich, it's earthy, it's cheesy and crisp and a little bit hot, and it's just plain delicious. Your friends will be asking you to make this one every time they come over, no matter what else is on the menu.

Serves 4 as a side dish

THE INGREDIENTS

4oz (115g) bacon, diced small
1½lb (675g) white mushrooms, stems trimmed
¼ cup olive oil
1 tablespoon minced fresh garlic
1 teaspoon red pepper flakes
Kosher salt and freshly cracked black pepper to taste
¼ cup grated parmesan cheese
¼ cup roughly chopped fresh parsley
2 tablespoons unsalted butter, softened

On the stove top, cook the bacon until crisp in a sauté pan over medium heat (6–8 minutes). Drain well and set aside.

Build a fire in your grill. When the coals are all ignited, the flames have died down, and the temperature is medium (*see p34*), you're ready to cook.

Combine the mushrooms, olive oil, garlic, red pepper flakes, and salt and pepper in a bowl and toss until evenly coated. If the mushrooms are small, thread them onto skewers. Put the mushrooms on the grill directly over the coals and cook until they are moist all the way through—about 10 minutes. Put the mushrooms into a large bowl and immediately add the bacon, parmesan, parsley, and butter, tossing gently until the mushrooms are evenly coated with butter and cheese. If necessary, season with more salt and pepper to taste, and serve immediately.

GRILLED PORTOBELLO MUSHROOMS
WITH BUTTER AND GARLIC

Portobello mushrooms should be a staple of every griller's repertoire. Large enough so they are easy to handle on the grill, full of that deep, rich, earthy flavor that we love in mushrooms, and these days very widely available, they are a great option for a quick but elegant side dish. Just sear them on the grill, toss them with a little butter, garlic, and parsley, and you're there.

Serves 4 to 6 as a side dish

THE INGREDIENTS

6 Portobello mushrooms, as large as you can find
   (about 2lb/900g in total), stems removed
3 tablespoons olive oil
Kosher salt and freshly cracked black pepper
6 tablespoons unsalted butter, at room temperature
1 tablespoon minced fresh garlic
¼ cup roughly chopped fresh parsley

Build a fire in your grill. When the coals are all ignited, the flames have died down, and the temperature is medium (*see p34*), you're ready to cook.

Rub the mushrooms with oil and sprinkle them generously with salt and pepper, then put them on the grill directly over the coals and cook until they are tender and slightly seared (6–8 minutes per side). If you want to check for doneness, cut into one of the mushrooms to be sure it is moist all the way through, rather than dry at the center.

As soon as the mushrooms are done, cut them into thick slices and place them in a bowl. Top the hot mushrooms with the butter and garlic, tossing gently to coat them all over. Transfer to a serving dish, garnish with parsley, and serve immediately.

GRILLED SHIITAKE MUSHROOMS
WITH SCALLIONS AND GINGER

Like Portobellos (*see facing page*), shiitake mushrooms seem made for the grill. As with most foods, we think they're best teamed with flavors from their region of origin, so here we toss them with a simple Asian-style dressing right as they come off the grill; that way, they absorb the flavors quickly.

Serves 4 to 6 as a side dish

THE MUSHROOMS

2lb (900g) large fresh shiitake mushrooms, tough bottom part of stems trimmed off

Kosher salt and freshly cracked black pepper

1 tablespoon Asian sesame oil

1 tablespoon vegetable oil

THE DRESSING

3 tablespoons soy sauce

2 tablespoons dry sherry

1 tablespoon Asian sesame oil

1 tablespoon peeled and minced fresh ginger

THE GARNISH

2 tablespoons thinly sliced scallions, white and light green parts

Build a fire in your grill. When the coals are all ignited, the flames have died down, and the temperature is medium-hot (*see p34*), you're ready to cook.

Combine the dressing ingredients in a small bowl, mix well, and set aside.

Place the mushrooms in a large bowl, sprinkle generously with salt and pepper, and drizzle with the sesame and vegetable oils, tossing to coat. Put them on the grill directly over the coals and cook until they are browned and crisp and have grill marks on them (3–4 minutes per side). If you want to check for doneness, cut into one of the mushrooms to be sure it is moist all the way through, rather than dry at the center.

When the mushrooms are done, return them to the bowl you originally tossed them in, add the dressing, and toss gently to coat. Transfer the mushrooms to a serving dish, garnish with the scallions, and serve.

GRILLED BUFFALO ASPARAGUS

Asparagus, quite delicious grilled all by itself, is also a very adaptable vegetable, compatible with a wide range of flavorings that actually bring out, rather than mask, its subtle but distinctive taste. Okay, so you might think that the "buffalo" approach, with the intensity of hot sauce and blue cheese, is going too far. You might think so, but you would be wrong. Somehow these flavors all work together, and this is one of the most popular side dishes we've come up with recently. It also makes an excellent appetizer.

Serves 4 as a side dish

THE INGREDIENTS

24 asparagus spears, slightly larger in diameter than
   a pencil, trimmed
2 tablespoons olive oil
Kosher salt and freshly cracked black pepper
¼ cup of your favorite hot sauce
3 tablespoons soft butter
¼ cup blue cheese

Build a fire in your grill. When the coals are all ignited, the flames have died down, and the temperature is medium (*see p34*), you're ready to cook.

Rub the asparagus with oil and sprinkle generously with salt and pepper, then put on the grill directly over the coals (you can use skewers to keep them together if you wish). Cook until the spears are browned and tender (4–6 minutes).

Combine the hot sauce and butter in a large bowl, mashing until smooth. Add the asparagus and toss gently to coat with the sauce.

Arrange the asparagus on a serving platter, crumble the blue cheese over the top, and serve.

SIPS AND SWEETS

TO DO YOUR BEST WORK AT THE GRILL, IT HELPS
TO HAVE A FAVORITE BEVERAGE CLOSE AT HAND.
AND OF COURSE, YOU'LL WANT TO PROVIDE SOME
FOR YOUR GUESTS, TOO. SO HERE THEY ARE,
ALONG WITH A HANDFUL OF SWEET ENDINGS TO
COMPLETE THE MEAL. NEVER THOUGHT OF
DOING DESSERTS ON THE GRILL? THINK AGAIN.

GRILLED MANGOES WITH ICE CREAM AND HOMEMADE STRAWBERRY SAUCE

We love grilled fruit, but until recently we hadn't really figured out a good way to grill mangoes, one of our favorites. This method works well, and it creates a very unusual dessert that most of our friends really like. It can be a bit of a mess to eat, though—if that bothers you, just slice the chunks of mango into a bowl when they are cool enough after grilling, then add the ice cream and strawberry sauce.

Serves 4

THE INGREDIENTS

2 cups fresh strawberries, washed, hulled, and quartered
1 tablespoon granulated sugar
1 teaspoon fresh lime juice
2 ripe but firm mangoes
2 tablespoons unsalted butter, melted
1 quart (1 liter) really good vanilla ice cream, or other flavor of your choice

Build a fire in your grill. When the coals are all ignited, the flames have died down, and the temperature is medium (*see p34*), you're ready to cook.

Combine the strawberries, sugar, and lime juice in a bowl and mix well, mushing the berries up just a bit as you mix.

Cut the two halves away from the pit of each mango. For each half, crosshatch the flesh without piercing the skin, then, with your thumbs at the center of the skin side, press each half inside-out so that it looks sort of like a porcupine. Brush the cut sides of the mango halves lightly with butter, then put them on the grill directly over the coals, cut side down, and cook until golden brown (6–8 minutes). Flip them over, brush the flesh lightly with butter again, and cook until the butter just starts to caramelize (2–3 minutes more).

Place the hot, grilled mangoes cut side up on dessert plates, top each with a scoop of ice cream, and spoon the strawberry sauce over the top.

ASH-ROASTED PEARS WITH VANILLA, TOASTED ALMONDS, AND CINNAMON WHIPPED CREAM

As long as you've got the fire going, why not use the coals to cook dessert? This one—pears stuffed with butter and almonds and topped with flavored whipped cream—is ideal for fall, when pears are at their peak.

Serves 6

THE INGREDIENTS

½ cup almonds
6 large, firm Bosc pears
6 tablespoons unsalted butter, cut into 6 pieces
1 tablespoon vanilla extract
1 cup well chilled heavy cream
¼ cup powdered sugar
½ teaspoon ground cinnamon

Toast the almonds in a shallow baking pan in a 350°F (180°C) oven for 5–10 minutes, or very carefully in a dry skillet on the grill, shaking frequently to avoid burning, until golden (3–5 minutes). Chop them finely in a food processor or coffee grinder.

Core the pears through the top, stopping ¼in (3mm) from the bottom. Push 1 tablespoon of butter into the center of each pear, along with about ⅙ of the almonds and ½ teaspoon vanilla.

For each pear, stack up 4 sheets of heavy-duty foil, each about 2ft (60cm) long. Place the pears in the center of the top sheets of foil, then fold up the sheets around each pear one after the other, turning the package a quarter-turn each time and making sure that each sheet is well sealed around the pear.

Place the foil-wrapped pears in the coals at the periphery of the fire, where the heat is less intense. Draw the coals up around the packages and cook until the pears are tender (15–20 minutes).

While the pears are roasting, combine the cream, sugar, and cinnamon in a deep bowl. Beat with an electric mixer on medium-high speed until soft peaks form.

When the pears are tender, remove them from the coals and peel back the foil. Top each pear with a big spoonful of whipped cream and serve warm.

ASH-ROASTED APPLES WITH BLUE CHEESE-DATE STUFFING AND CINNAMON-ORANGE CARAMEL SAUCE

This dessert—cooked in the coals while dinner is grilling—is an extreme version of baked apples, complete with a tangy-sweet stuffing and a luscious caramel sauce. If you like, you can skip the sauce; on the other hand, you can make it hours ahead of time and just stick it in the microwave (or warm it up in a saucepan over very low heat) right before serving dessert.

Serves 4

THE APPLES

¼ cup pecans
4 large Golden Delicious apples (or other firm apples such as Jonathans, Braeburns, Empires, or Romes)
8oz (225g) blue cheese, crumbled
¼ cup diced pitted dates

THE SAUCE

½ cup granulated sugar
Juice of ½ orange (about ¼ cup)
3in (7.5cm) cinnamon stick
¼ cup heavy cream
Grated zest of ½ orange
Pinch salt

Toast the pecans in a shallow baking pan in a 350°F (180°C) oven for 5–10 minutes, or very carefully in a dry skillet on the grill, shaking frequently to avoid burning, until golden (3–5 minutes). Chop them finely in a food processor or coffee grinder.

Core the apples through the top, stopping ½in (1cm) from the bottom. Combine the cheese, dates, and pecans in a bowl and mix gently until evenly combined. Push a quarter of the mixture into the center of each apple.

For each apple, stack up 4 sheets of heavy-duty foil, each about 2ft (60cm) long. Place the apples in the center of the top sheets of foil, then fold up the sheets around each apple one after the other, turning the package a quarter-turn each time and making sure that each sheet is well sealed around the apple.

Place the foil-wrapped apples in the coals at the periphery of the fire, where the heat is less intense. Pile the coals up around the packages and cook until the apples are tender (20–30 minutes).

While the apples are roasting, combine the sugar and orange juice in a small saucepan over medium heat, stirring just until the sugar dissolves and the mixture comes to a boil. Add the cinnamon stick and simmer without stirring until the syrup turns deep amber—about 5 minutes. Remove from the heat and immediately add the cream, orange zest, and salt—the mixture will steam and sputter, and the caramel will congeal. Continue to cook, stirring gently, until the caramel dissolves completely. Set aside.

When the apples are tender, remove the packages from the coals and cut open the foil. Remove the cinnamon stick from the caramel and drizzle the warm sauce over the apples.

GRILLED BANANA UPSIDE-DOWN CAKE

Grilled bananas bring a sweet, slightly smoky, caramelized flavor to the "topping" of this twist on a classic, created by our friend and collaborator Kirsten Mikalson. Ground pecans add a little body to the cake's texture and a rich, nutty taste. If you're feeling particularly decadent, try serving this warm with a scoop of *dulce de leche* ice cream.

Serves 6 to 8

THE CAKE

¼ cup pecans

1 cup all-purpose flour

2 teaspoons baking powder

¼ teaspoon salt

Pinch ground cinnamon

6 tablespoons unsalted butter, room temperature

¾ cup granulated sugar

1 large egg

1 large egg white

½ teaspoon vanilla extract

6 tablespoons whole milk

THE TOPPING

3 ripe but firm bananas, unpeeled, halved lengthwise

½ cup firmly packed soft light brown sugar

¼ cup maple syrup

3 tablespoons unsalted butter, plus 1 tablespoon for buttering the pan

¼ teaspoon ground allspice

Pinch salt

Preheat the oven to 350°F (180°C). Generously butter a 9in (23cm) cake pan. Build a fire in your grill. When the coals are all ignited, the flames have died down, and the temperature is medium-hot (*see p34*), you're ready to cook.

For the topping: Place the bananas on the grill over the coals, cut side down, and cook until golden brown and slightly charred (2–3 minutes). Set aside.

Combine the rest of the topping ingredients in a small saucepan and, on the stove top, bring the mixture to a full boil over medium-high heat, stirring until melted and smooth. Cook for 1 minute, then pour into the buttered cake pan. Peel the bananas and arrange them, grilled side down, on the syrup. Set aside.

Toast the pecans in a shallow baking pan in the oven for 5–10 minutes. Grind in a food processor or coffee grinder. Combine the ground pecans, flour, baking powder, salt, and cinnamon in a bowl and mix well.

Combine the butter and sugar in a large mixing bowl and beat until creamy. Add the egg, egg white, and vanilla; beat until light and fluffy (about 1 minute), scraping down the bowl as necessary. Add half the dry ingredients; beat on medium speed until well blended. Add the milk and mix well, scraping down the sides of bowl. Add the remaining dry ingredients and beat until well blended. Spoon the batter over the bananas, smoothing the surface. Bake until a toothpick inserted into the center of the cake comes out clean (about 30 minutes).

Run a knife around the sides of the pan to loosen. Set the pan on a wire rack and let the cake cool for 15 minutes. Invert the cake onto a serving plate and carefully lift off the pan. Serve warm or at room temperature.

GRILLED TROPICAL PINEAPPLE AND BANANAS FOSTER

We've always liked Bananas Foster, the modern classic dessert created at Brennan's Restaurant in New Orleans. So we decided to take it in a more tropical direction by adding coconut and pineapple. And, of course, we grill the fruit. We think that the subtle smoky dimension that this brings to the dish really takes it to another level.

Serves 4

THE INGREDIENTS

2 bananas, unpeeled, halved lengthwise, then halved crosswise

2 slices fresh pineapple, each ½in (1cm) thick, peeled, halved, and cored

2 tablespoons vegetable oil

½ cup soft dark brown sugar

4 tablespoons butter

¼ teaspoon cinnamon

¼ cup banana liqueur

½ cup your favorite dark rum

1 lime, cut in half

1 pint (500ml) your favorite ice cream

¼ cup toasted shredded coconut (optional)

Build a fire in your grill. When the coals are all ignited, the flames have died down, and the temperature is medium (*see p34*), you're ready to cook.

Rub the banana and pineapple slices lightly with oil and arrange them, bananas cut side down, on the grill over the coals. Cook until the bananas are golden and the pineapple slices have light grill marks—about 2 minutes per side. Peel the bananas once cool enough to handle.

Combine the brown sugar, butter, and cinnamon in a large skillet, and place it on the stove top over medium heat. When the butter and sugar are melted and very hot, mix well and add the grilled pineapple slices and peeled bananas to the skillet, turning in the syrup to coat. Add the liqueur and rum, and as soon as the mixture starts to boil, wave a long, lit match above the surface of the syrup to ignite. Baste the fruit with the syrup until the flames die out, and immediately squeeze the lime halves over the skillet.

Spoon the hot fruit and syrup over bowls of ice cream, sprinkle with coconut, and serve.

GRILLED BALSAMIC-GLAZED PEACHES
WITH GOAT CHEESE

Add a bit of sugar and black pepper to the inexpensive balsamic vinegar found in supermarkets, boil it down it until it's syrupy, and you've got yourself an easy but complex-tasting sauce. Combine this with grilled peaches and some tangy goat cheese, and the result is a quick dessert that will knock your guests' socks off with its depth of flavor.

Serves 4

THE INGREDIENTS

1 cup balsamic vinegar
2 tablespoons granulated sugar
1 tablespoon freshly cracked black pepper
2 ripe but firm large peaches, halved and pitted
2 tablespoons vegetable oil
4oz (115g) goat cheese, crumbled

Combine the vinegar, sugar, and pepper in a small saucepan and, on the stove top, bring the mixture to a boil, stirring occasionally. Reduce the heat and simmer vigorously until the mixture is syrupy and reduced by about two-thirds in volume (25–30 minutes). Remove from the heat and set aside.

Build a fire in your grill. When the coals are all ignited, the flames have died down, and the temperature is medium (*see p34*), you're ready to cook.

Rub the peach halves lightly with oil, then put them on the grill directly over the coals, cut side down, and cook just until lightly seared—about 6 minutes. Flip them over, brush them generously with the glaze, and cook for 2–3 minutes more.

Place the peaches cut side up on dessert plates and immediately top each one with a spoonful of goat cheese. Drizzle with some additional glaze if desired, and serve warm.

POMEGRANATE LEMONADE

When you're having a cookout and you're looking for a refreshing non-alcoholic drink that will appeal to adults, try this. The pomegranate juice adds a depth and complexity of flavor without dulling the uniquely compelling sour-sweet taste of classic lemonade.

Makes about 2 quarts (2 liters)

1 cup granulated sugar
½ cup water
Juice of 8 lemons (about 2 cups)

1 cup fresh or bottled pomegranate juice
1 quart (1 liter) cold water
Mint sprigs to garnish (optional)

In a small saucepan, combine the sugar and ½ cup water. Bring to a boil, stirring frequently, then lower the heat and simmer until the sugar is fully dissolved (about 1 minute). Remove from the heat and let cool to room temperature.

Fill a large pitcher halfway with ice. Add the lemon juice, pomegranate juice, cold water, and cooled syrup, and mix well.

To serve, fill tall glasses halfway with ice, and pour the lemonade over. Garnish with mint sprigs if desired.

MANGO LIMEADE

Mango juice and fresh mango give a kick of tropical flavor to traditional limeade. Although the mango is sweet, it has a kind of slightly funky flavor that keeps the drink from being too saccharine. This is a good drink for when there are a bunch of kids around—they will love it, plus they can help you squeeze all those limes.

Makes about 2 quarts (2 liters)

1 cup granulated sugar
½ cup water
Juice of 16 limes (about 2 cups)
1 cup mango juice

1 quart (1 liter) cold water
1 cup diced mango
Cilantro sprigs to garnish (optional)

In a small saucepan, combine the sugar and water. Bring to a boil, stirring frequently, then lower the heat and simmer until the sugar is fully dissolved (about 1 minute). Remove from the heat and let cool to room temperature.

Fill a large pitcher halfway with ice. Add the lime juice, mango juice, cold water, and cooled syrup and mix well.

To serve, fill tall glasses halfway with ice, and top each with some of the diced mango. Pour the limeade over, and garnish with cilantro sprigs if desired.

WATERMELON MOJITO

In our opinion, watermelon makes any summer drink more refreshing, and the mojito is no exception. This is a welcome drink before any grilled dinner, but we think it's especially delicious before any meal with Latin flavors.

Makes 1 drink

20 fresh mint leaves, a few reserved for garnishing

2 tablespoons chopped fresh watermelon (without seeds), plus a small wedge to garnish

Juice of 1 lime (about 2 tablespoons)

1 tablespoon granulated sugar

2oz (60ml) light rum

3oz (90ml) soda water

Put the mint leaves, watermelon, lime juice, and sugar in a tall glass and mash them together until the mint leaves are well bruised and the watermelon is crushed (1–2 minutes). Fill the glass with ice cubes, pour in the rum, and mix well. Top with the soda water, and garnish with a watermelon wedge and reserved mint leaves.

LYCHEE COCKTAIL

The delicate, floral sweetness of the lychee is one of Asia's most alluring flavors, so we figured it would be an excellent base for an unusual and very refreshing cocktail. You know what? We were right. This drink is particularly nice for summer parties.

Makes 1 drink

5 canned lychees, plus 1 tablespoon juice from the can

2oz (60ml) vodka

1oz (30ml) Grand Marnier

Juice of ½ lime (about a tablespoon)

4 mint leaves

Combine four of the lychees with the lychee juice, vodka, Grand Marnier, lime juice, mint leaves, and ice cubes in a cocktail shaker, and shake until the mixture is thoroughly combined and well chilled (20–30 seconds). Strain into a martini glass, garnish with the remaining lychee, and serve.

EAST COAST GRILL SANGRIA

One of the most popular summer drinks at the East Coast Grill, this is a pretty straightforward version of the super-refreshing Spanish drink combining red wine and fruit, with some triple sec and brandy to deepen the flavor and add a little bit more of a kick. Bring a pitcher of this out to sip while you're grilling, and you and your guests are all going to be very happy.

Makes about 8 glasses

Plenty of ice cubes
1 bottle (750ml) dry red wine such as Beaujolais, Chianti, or Pinot Noir
Juice of 2 oranges (about 1 cup)
4oz (120ml) triple sec

4oz (120ml) brandy
¼ cup granulated sugar
1 orange (unpeeled), sliced into thin rounds, rounds cut in half
8oz (240ml) club soda

Fill a large pitcher halfway with ice, then pour in the wine, orange juice, triple sec, brandy, and sugar. Add the orange slices and stir until the sugar dissolves and the mixture is very cold.

Pour the sangria into glasses, top each drink with a splash of soda, and serve.

PINK SANGRIA WITH PEACHES

We've come to like rosé wines a lot lately, primarily because it's become so much easier to find good-quality ones. This combination of rosé and peaches, with citrus zing and a bit of triple sec, has got to be one of the lightest, most refreshing, but still fully satisfying drinks you'll have all summer. (Some of our friends even like it in the fall and spring.)

Makes about 8 glasses

3 ripe but firm peaches, halved and pitted
Plenty of ice cubes
1 bottle (750ml) dry rosé wine
Juice of 2 oranges (about 1 cup)

Juice of 1 lime (about 2 tablespoons)
4oz (120ml) triple sec
8oz (240ml) club soda

Dice two of the peaches small and cut the third one into eight thin wedges. Fill a large pitcher halfway with ice, then pour in the wine, orange juice, lime juice, and triple sec. Add half the diced peaches and stir until the sugar dissolves and the mixture is very cold.

Pour the sangria into glasses and add the remaining diced fruit. Top each drink with a generous splash of soda, garnish with a peach wedge, and serve.

BLUE MARGARITA

This visually arresting cocktail may well have been responsible for starting the margarita craze when it first took hold back in the early '80s. No one is quite sure who originated it, but one thing about it is certain: It may look a little odd, but it tastes great.

Makes 1 drink

¼ cup coarse salt (optional)
2oz (60ml) good-quality tequila
Juice of 2 limes (about ¼ cup), squeezed rinds
   reserved

1oz (30ml) blue Curaçao
1 teaspoon granulated sugar
1 lime slice to garnish

If you want your margarita glass salted, do it now: Spread the salt in a saucer or shallow dish. Rub the rim of the glass with the reserved lime rinds (from making the juice), then dip the rim into the salt.

Fill the glass about halfway with ice.

Combine the tequila, lime juice, blue Curaçao, sugar, and ice cubes in a cocktail shaker, and shake until the mixture is thoroughly combined and well chilled (20–30 seconds). Strain into the ice-filled glass and garnish with a slice of lime. Serve immediately.

CLASSIC DARK AND STORMY

The history of this ultra-simple but very delicious drink is—well, I suppose you could say it's dark and stormy. No one's quite sure where it originated, but today it's claimed as the national drink of Bermuda, and is popular in tropical locations around the world. The rich, molasses-y, licoricey flavor of Gosling's makes it our favorite rum for this drink, but you can use any dark rum you happen to have around.

Makes 1 drink

2oz (60ml) Gosling's or other dark rum
4oz (120ml) ginger beer
Lime wedge to garnish

Fill a tall glass about halfway with ice cubes and pour in the dark rum. Add the ginger beer, mix well, garnish with the wedge of lime, and serve.

HOT LIPS MARGARITA

We make every kind of margarita at the East Coast Grill, but this one has become a big favorite. Adding a few slices of jalapeño to the mix before you shake it up imparts just the right trace of heat without rendering it undrinkably fiery.

Makes 1 drink

¼ cup coarse salt (optional)
2oz (60ml) good-quality tequila
Juice of 2 limes (about ¼ cup), squeezed rinds reserved
1oz (30ml) triple sec

5 thin slices of red or green jalapeño pepper, or other fresh chile of your choice
1 teaspoon granulated sugar
1 lime slice to garnish

If you want your margarita glass salted, do it now: Spread the salt in a saucer or shallow dish. Rub the rim of the glass with the reserved lime rinds (from making the juice), then dip the rim into the salt.

Fill the glass about halfway with ice.

Combine the tequila, lime juice, triple sec, jalapeño slices, sugar, and ice cubes in a cocktail shaker, and shake until the mixture is thoroughly combined and well chilled (20–30 seconds). Strain into the ice-filled glass and garnish with a slice of lime. Serve immediately.

GREEN GRAPE CAIPIRINHA

Not many years ago, cachaça, the distilled sugar cane liquor of Brazil, was popular only in that country, where per capita consumption runs about three gallons per year. But the recent popularity of the caipirinha cocktail has given this liquor a worldwide reputation. Here we substitute green grapes for the lime used in the traditional version, which gives a slightly sweeter, more subtle flavor.

Makes 1 drink

8 green grapes, halved
1½ tablespoons granulated sugar
2oz (60ml) cachaça

Combine the grapes and sugar in an old-fashioned glass and mash them together until the grapes are pretty well smashed (at least 1 minute). Fill the glass with ice cubes, pour in the cachaça, mix well, and serve.

INDEX

ACKNOWLEDGMENTS

AUTHORS' ACKNOWLEDGMENTS

FROM BOTH OF US

Thanks to our inimitable agent, the indefatigable Doe Coover, who keeps finding new avenues for us to ply our trade. Also, thanks to Kirsten Mikalson and Nancy Boyce who were indispensable aides in transfering the recipes in this book from mind to paper. And to all the folks at DK and Cobalt, in particular Louise Abbott, for putting together a beautiful book that actually makes sense. And, of course, thanks to Rick and Susan, Tommy, Lizzie, and Josh, and Owen T.

FROM CHRIS

To own a restaurant and be able to do anything but run the restaurant 24/7 is a luxury that is not afforded to most folks in the business. To my good fortune, at the East Coast Grill I work with a group of people whose diligence, dedication, and hard work allow me to pursue projects outside of the restaurant. To them I say: you are awesome, thanks for making me look good, and don't go changin'. Special shout-outs to Chefs Eric Gburski and Jason Lord, General Manager Kristi Morris, and CFO Laurie Govoni.

Collaborating on a book is an arduous task in any event, but over my cookbook-writing career I have been privileged to work with the accomplished wordsmith, Doc Willoughby, whose sharp eye, quick wit, and cool Manhattan apartment make for a pleasurable partnership. Doc, you always do more than your share of the work without too much complaning. Thanks for that and thanks for the laughs.

FROM DOC

Thanks to Ruth, Larry, and all the other folks at *Gourmet* for their patience and forbearance as I worked my way through this book. And to Mark Bittman for helping me keep perspective on the whole thing. Thanks, too, to my faithful dining companions Tucker, Chris I, Francis, Richard, and Bobby, and to Dave for keeping me from getting too fat.

Creating books with my friend Chris has always been as much fun as it is work. His lifelong slogan, "Work smarter, not harder," translates into more exciting dinners and cool excursions than a cookbook author has any right to expect. Not to mention that his recipes rock. Thanks, Chris, for your good humor, sense of adventure, and steadfast friendship.

PUBLISHER'S ACKNOWLEDGMENTS

Cobalt id would like to thank the following for their help with this book: Sarah Tomley for editorial assistance; Christy Lusiak and Charles Wills for proofreading and US liaison; and Hilary Bird for indexing. Our thanks also to Briar Towers at Dorling Kindersley, and especially to Ian O'Leary, photography assistant Gemma Reynolds, and stylist Gizzi Erskine, who is represented by HERS (hersagency.co.uk).